THE STORY
OF THE MONGOLS WHOM
WE CALL THE TARTARS

HISTORIA MONGALORUM QUOS NOS TARTAROS APPELLAMUS

Friar Giovanni Di Plano Carpini's
Account of his Embassy
to the Court of the Mongol Khan

Translated by
Erik Hildinger

BRANDEN PUBLISHING COMPANY
Boston

Library of Congress Cataloging-in-Publication Data

Giovanni, da Pian del Carpine, Archbishop of
Antivari, d. 1252.
  [Historia Mongolorum. English]
  The story of the Mongols whom we call the
Tartars = Historia Mongalorum quos nos Tartaros
appellamus : Friar Giovanni di Plano Carpini's
account of his embassy to the court of the Mongol
Khan / translated by Erik Hildinger.
      p.   cm.
  Includes bibliographic references and index.
  ISBN 0-8283-2017-9 (pbk.)
  1. Mongols--History.
  2. Asia--Description and travel.

  I. Title.
  DS6.G5413 1996
  950'.04942--dc20   96-940
                                           CIP

BRANDEN PUBLISHING COMPANY, Inc.
17 Station Street
Box 843 Brookline Village
Boston, MA 02147

THE STORY OF THE MONGOLS

Contents

PREFACE

The modern state of Mongolia lies to the west and north of China. Seven hundred years ago those who spoke the Mongol language, Tungisic in origin, also lived on the steppes further north and west in what is now Russia and Siberia, and many still do. These Asian people competed for a living with their more numerous Turkic-speaking cousins and their occasional incursions into the civilized lands surrounding the steppes had generally had horrifying consequences for sedentary nations.

The Mongols were a nomadic people living from their herds and flocks. Thus they moved between two areas summer and winter, to find grazing for the animals. Their homes were (and some still are) *gers*, round felt tents easily disassembled or moved from place to place. They travelled by horse which had first been domesticated in southern Russia perhaps three thousand five hundred years ago. They fought interminably among themselves and the bow was their weapon-- metal is hard to work and scarce in the steppe. In any case they were superb archers.

Mongol society, like that of other steppe peoples, was simple. The religion was shamanistic, an ancient and primitive belief in a multitude of spirits such as is found in northern Asia and among the natives of the Americas who had crossed the Bering straight from Asia so long before.

The steppe has three distinct areas. To the north a forested belt, then the great grasslands, and finally the desert regions. The better areas were the object of constant struggles among the steppe tribes, whether Mongols, Turks, Merkits, Tatars, Naimans, or any of a dozen nations who are only names today. The trigger of such a conflict might be a political shift among the tribes, or a period of drought, a common occurrence on the steppe, which caused one tribe to seek better territory at the expense of another. Thus, every man was, of necessity, a warrior. War is the profession of the steppe and, among pre-industrial peoples, no one is better at it. Europe knew this from the incursions of the Huns and Magyars in the fifth and eighth centuries; it was revisited by this scourge in the thirteenth, and it was stunned.

In April 1241 Mongol armies had killed some one hundred thousand European knights and men-at-arms in Poland and Hungary. They had beaten every western army they had come against. Henry II of Silesia was dead, Boleslav IV, Count of the Poles, was in hiding, and the kingdom of Hungary no longer existed; its king, Bela IV, was fleeing to the Adriatic coast pursued by a Mongol army determined to kill him. As for the country itself, the Mongols began to systematically strip and depopulate it and to strike coins. It belonged to Batu, grandson of Jinghiz Khan, the Emperor of All Men.

Meanwhile, Pope Gregory IX and the Holy Roman Emperor Frederick II prepared to continue their personal war while Mongol scouts approached Venice. There was no army the Europeans could muster to oppose them. There seemed no reason to suppose that western Europe would not suffer the fate of central Europe and Russia.

In February 1241 the Mongol army had left its base in southern Russia and begun to cross the frozen rivers into central Europe. It consisted of about seventy thousand men, all of them cavalry. Nominally commanded by Batu, a grandson of Jinghiz Khan, he was guided by his grandfather's famous lieutenant, Subotai, a brilliant campaigner. This general had commanded in the campaigns against the Northern Sung of China and had helped in the destruction of the Kwarizmian Empire. He had planned the campaign against Europe for a year and the results would show.

The Mongols had defeated every major Russian principality and had spent a year resting and regrouping in what is now the Ukraine before crossing into central Europe. Their target was Hungary, though to achieve its defeat the Mongols wished to remove opposition from other quarters. To that end the Mongol army was divided into two unequal forces. The smaller part of about thirty thousand men started off first at the beginning of March and went north into Poland to draw off any support for Hungary that might be found there. It was commanded by two of Jinghiz Khan's grandsons, Baidar and Kaadan, and swept in a northward arc past the edge of the Carpathians and into Poland. The larger army of about forty thousand advanced under the command of Subotai and Batu a few days later and was itself broken into two contingents each of which entered the Carpathians by a different route and crossed into Hungary.

Mongols scouts were seen ranging Poland and Hungary and the European nobility began to muster armies. Count Boleslav IV of Poland, one of several lords who claimed to be its king, assembled one. It consisted of Polish knights, foreign knights from as far away as France and Germany, and members of the military orders. These last, such as the Knights Templar and the Hospitallers were monks who submitted to rigid personal discipline and fought as knights for the protection of the church. They were Europe's most disciplined and professional soldiers. This army numbered about thirty thousand.

Duke Henry of Silesia drew up a similar, somewhat larger army. To the south, King Bela of Hungary gathered his forces, but found it difficult as his nobles mistrusted his power and were uncooperative.

The Mongol column which had gone north began to search for resistance in Poland. Baidar and Kaadan were aware of Duke Henry's army and determined to meet and prevent it supporting Bela in Hungary in his contest with Batu and Subotai. Far to the south Subotai and Batu's forces approached the guarded Hungarian passes of the Carpathians.

After slow going in the snow for a few weeks the northern column under Baidar and Kaadan split into two. On March 18 they met the first resistance, the combined armies of Boleslav and Prince Mieceslas. The Mongols split the Europeans apart at the battle, the Poles heading south, the Slavs west. The Mongols then swept ahead to Kracow from which the inhabitants were fleeing; they burnt the city. This done, they tossed a bridge across the Oder and took Breslau only to discover that the Duke Henry of Silesia had gathered his army near Liegnitz, now Legnica in modern Poland. Henry's army numbered about forty thousand and awaited support from a Bohemian army of fifty thousand under King Wenceslas. The Mongols were outnumbered and knew of Wenceslas's approach. Baidar and Kaadan decided to attack at once before the western armies could join.

Meanwhile, in Hungary, King Bela had thought to stop the Mongol advance by cutting trees across the paths in the Carpathian mountains and by strengthening the fortress garrisons which defended the passes. He used the time he supposed he had gained to contend with his nobles and prepare for the campaign. On March 10 he received news that the Mongols, or Tartars as he knew them, had begun to attack the passes. Four days later Nador Denes, the commander of the passes arrived to announce that they had fallen and that the Mongols were advancing. Indeed they were. They came down the mountains covering forty miles a day in the snow, a speed unlike anything the Hungarians had ever seen. Bela began to marshal his army in the German town of Pesth across the Danube from his fortress at Buda.

In Poland, Duke Henry and his Polish-German army left the safety of Liegnitz on the morning of April 9 to try to join up with Wenceslas. Instead they were confronted by the Mongol army on a plain south of Liegnitz, a place afterwards called the "Wahlstatt", or chosen place. The Europeans took up positions on level ground and prepared to fight. Their army, made up of both knights and infantry was arrayed in conventional fashion with the mounted soldiers in the van and the infantry behind.

When the engagement began the Europeans were disconcerted at the enemy's moving without battle cries or trumpets-- all signals were given by pennant and standard. It was difficult to gauge the Mongols' numbers: their formations were denser than those of the knights and they appeared half as numerous as in fact they were. The first of Duke Henry's divisions charged and was beaten back by Mongol arrows. The heavily armored knights not only could not close with the lightly equipped horse archers, they were driven into a retreat.

A second charge followed. This one, unlike the first, seemed successful, the Mongols fleeing before the knights. Encouraged, the knights pressed on their attack, eager to meet the Mongols with lance and broadsword. The enemy continued to melt away before them, evidently unable to face the charge of such heavy horsemen. However, things were not as they seemed; the knights had fallen victim to the steppe tactic of the feigned retreat. The Mongols, unlike the knights, had been taught to retreat as a tactical move and as they did so they drew the knights into a line separated from the infantry. The Mongols then swept to either side of the knights who were strung out, and showered them with arrows from their powerful composite bows. Other Mongols lay in ambush, prepared to meet the knights as they fell into the trap. Where the Mongols found the knights' armor effective against their arrows they simply shot horses. The dismounted knights were then easy prey for the Mongols who ran them down with lance or saber with little danger to themselves.

There was a final trick: smoke drifted across the battlefield between the infantry and the knights who had charged ahead so that neither force could see the other. The Europeans suspected sorcery and this explanation is found in the chronicles. The Mongols slaughtered the Europeans on their own terms and virtually annihilated them. Duke Henry was killed trying to escape and, following a Mongol custom used to count the dead, an ear was cut from each dead European. The Mongols filled nine sacks with ears. Contemporary records state twenty-five to thirty thousand of Henry's men were killed.

Wenceslas and the Bohemians prudently halted their approach and retreated to a defensive position. Baidar and Kaadan, satisfied that there was no longer any serious threat from Poland, headed south to Hungary to rejoin the other Mongol army.

On April 9, 1241, the very date of the Battle of Liegnitz, Bela left Pesth with his army of one hundred thousand to meet the Mongols who ravaged his country. Unlike Henry he would escape with his life, though for a time the Kingdom of Hungary would no longer exist.

The Hungarians advanced on the Mongols who retreated slowly ahead of them for several days. The retreat went on toward the plain of Mohi near the river Sajo where the Mongols pulled back further past woods beyond the opposite bank and disappeared. The Hungarian scouts could find no Mongols, only their horses' tracks.

Bela camped in the plain of Mohi and drew his wagons into a laager around the camp for protection. To his back and on either hand were woods. Should the Mongols wish to attack they would first have to cross the river to his front and there was only one bridge. Bela sent his brother Koloman, a capable soldier, to hold it with a thousand men.

Before light the Mongols had begun to move. They attacked the bridge, but were driven off. Meanwhile, though the Hungarians did not know it, other Mongols had moved upriver. The Mongols again attacked the bridge, but this time with catapults. Some reports tell of incendiary missiles pitched by these machines: flashing and smoking pots that disconcerted the Hungarians and drove them away. The Mongols took the bridge and by the time Bela could respond thousands of them had crossed the river ready to engage. The Hungarians charged into the mass of Mongols who, because they had little room to maneuver and were outnumbered and lightly armored, took a beating from the knights. The other Mongol force, led by Subotai, had meanwhile crossed the river unobserved. Batu received the Hungarian attack and then swept to the Hungarians' left flank, causing them to turn. Subotai appeared at the Hungarian rear. The Europeans had been completely outmaneuvered and they pulled back to their camp where the Mongols then attacked once more with catapults throwing burning tar and naphtha. As fires and smoke spread through the camp and it became more difficult to remain there, an odd thing happened: the Mongol army showed a gap to the west. Cautiously, a few of the Hungarians left the camp to escape through it. Those who went first were allowed to pass. Others followed. Many threw down their weapons and equipment to lighten their horses' loads for the run. More and more fled. The flight quickly became uncontrollable as the Hungarians tried to race back to Pesth, a hopeless task for the city was three days away. As they ran they became strung out like the knights who had chased Baidar and Kaadan's army during its feigned retreat in Poland. What had happened to the Poles and Germans happened to the Hungarians. The Mongols rode along their flanks and shot them with arrows or rode them down and killed them with lance and saber. This went on, some say, for two days. In the end as many as sixty-five thousand men had been killed. Bela escaped, unrecognized, and fled, ultimately to the Adriatic coast.

Eight months later, for no apparent reason, the Mongols pulled out of central Europe and did not return. The withdrawal was fortunate for the west; the Europeans never grasped who the Mongols were or how they fought. Another attack might have been even more disastrous. Very little would seem to have favored Europe in such a military contest. The Mongol Empire was a unified state stretching from northern China to the Ukraine while Europe was a patchwork of states at constant odds with each other.

The nominal leader of Europe, the Holy Roman Emperor Frederick II, never seemed particularly concerned by the Mongol threat. Frederick was called by his contemporaries *Stupor Mundi, or* "The Wonder of the World". A German by descent and master of most of the German world, his domains included his native Sicily where, in the thirteenth century, Greek was still spoken and where there was a significant Muslim population. Frederick spoke six languages fluently, among them Greek and Arabic. He got on well with Muslim rulers whom he considered his only cultural equals, he kept a harem, and was rumored to have written a book called *De Tribus Impostoribus,* or *About the Three Impostors.* These, so the story went, he considered to be Moses, Jesus and Muhammad. The story was false, but seems to have captured the essence of his views: it was said he did not to believe in God. Certainly he did not believe that he should be second to the pope. Furthermore he had led a crusade while excommunicated and freed Jerusalem by negotiation rather than bloodshed, something which incensed Pope Gregory.

Pope Gregory was as proud as Frederick and just as determined that papal authority should not be second to Frederick's secular authority. The two had fought a bitter war for years in Italy which was still unresolved in

1241 when the Mongols swept into Europe. In fact, it may be that Frederick saw the Mongols as a force to weaken the papacy to his advantage and so did little to address it. Pope Gregory would die shortly, though the rupture between the Papacy and the Holy Roman Empire persisted.

So while the rulers of Europe knew, before they first encountered them, that the Mongols were a terrible threat, they could not respond effectively. Refugees from the Russian principality of Kiev had fled west into Poland from their devastated country with horrifying stories. Everyone had been stunned when Kiev had fallen. The destruction was so appalling that five years later the papal envoy Giovanni di Plano Carpini described the area surrounding the city as covered with the skulls and bones of the slaughtered townspeople.

Pope Innocent IV succeeded to the papacy in 1243, on the heels of the Mongols' withdrawal from Hungary. These Tartars might return at any time: they were, after all, just over the Polish border, holding all of Russia as a vassal state, and no army had been able to offer them effective resistance either in Europe or Russia. What is more, no one really knew who they were, what their history was, what their religion was, or how far their lands extended. European knowledge of geography at the time was extremely limited. Even the proper name of the Tartars was not known.

Innocent had inherited Gregory's war with the Emperor; the last thing he needed was a Tartar invasion. He needed to learn the Tartars' intentions, so far as that was possible, and he needed to convince them to maintain peaceful relations with the west, if this were within his power. Therefore, he decided upon an emb-

1. Pope Innocent IV and his council
discussing the Mongol threat.

assy to Asia to offer baptism to the Khan. The idea of offering confirmation into a parochial religion to the most powerful man on earth, without his solicitation, must sound naive to us today, however, a medieval pope was not in the business of doubting God's power, and so perhaps the Khan might accept. Besides, Innocent may have known of the tolerance that Mongols showed to all religions and may have felt that a churchman might travel in relative safety. Then too, there were the Russians. A persistent concern of the papacy was the split between Catholicism and Orthodoxy, and a papal legate passing through orthodox lands could always try to reconcile the two churches. In fact, Prince Daniel of Galicia and Volhynia did agree to recognize the pope in the vain hope of western military help to free him from the Tartars.

So, on 16 April 1245 Brother Giovanni of Piano Carpini left Lyons at Pope Innocent IV's command on a journey to the dreaded Tartars. He would not return until November 1247. Explicitly, Carpini's mission was to offer baptism to the Tartars and tell them of Christianity. More important though, he was to observe them, find out their intentions, and report on them. He was in fact as much a spy as anything else. Brother Giovanni did as he was commanded and went to the Tartars with letters from the Pope. He could hardly have known, when he met Batu in Russia, that he would be sent three thousand miles further on into the heart of Central Asia to meet Guyuk, the Great Khan, the most powerful man in the world. When Carpini returned from his embassy more than a year later he wrote of his trip and that work, the *Historia Mongalorum,* is the first report by a European of a visit to Central Asia.

Giovanni di Plano Carpini was not a young man when he undertook his mission. Born around 1180, he was over sixty years old by this time, overweight, and must seem a strange man to choose for such a task. Upon a closer look, however, he was well suited. As a young man Carpini had joined the Franciscan Order established by Francis of Assisi in Carpini's native region. He had, in fact, been a personal follower of Francis and as his career in the church progressed, Carpini was entrusted with diplomatic missions to the court of the Holy Roman Emperor. At some point Carpini had also worked in Spain, probably as Provincial.

The greatest part of his career was spent in Germany, however, where he was sent in the 1220's. He was a warden in Saxony in 1222 and became Provincial of Germany in 1228. He established Franciscan monasteries and was well known to the rulers of that part of Europe. He spoke different languages, perhaps an eastern European one (though not, apparently, Russian or Ruthenian as we see from the *Historia*). He had one further advantage as a friar: unlike noble ambassadors he could more easily mingle with common people and win their confidence. This was important since Carpini's brief was to find out as much as he could about the Tartars, and this meant he was to find out about their religion, clothing, habits, military techniques, government, and even the extent of their empire. Clearly, Pope Innocent grasped that many things which ought to be known might best be found out by an unprepossessing man free to wander about among the people. It is difficult to emphasize how little was known of the Tartars before Carpini's expedition, but it was because of this ignorance that it was so important that the Pope's ambassador see and learn as much as he could. What was there to see? The was the largest land empire the world had ever known, stretching from northern China to Persia and up into the steppes of southern Russia to the frontier with Hungary. Compared with this the land extent of Europe was insignificant.

Though Europeans of Carpini's day referred to these people as Tartars at that time (a play on the Latin word for hell, *"Tartarus"*), they were more properly subjects of the Mongol Empire and would more often have been members of other, lesser known tribes from Central Asia. Carpini recognized this in the full title of his report, *Historia Mongalorum Quos Nos Tarataros Appellamus,* or *The Story of the Mongols Whom We Call the Tartars.* The Tartars, more properly the "Tatars", had been one of many steppe tribes defeated and amalgamated by the Mongols into their empire during the wars under their great leader Jinghiz Khan at the turn of the thirteenth century.

Jinghiz Khan (which seems to mean Oceanic or All Embracing Ruler) was born Temujin near Lake Baikal in what is now Russia around 1162 into a tribe of the Yekka Mongols. His name, derived from a Mongolian word for iron, suggests that his family may have had something to do, at one time at least, with metalwork. His father had been a khan, or chief, but had been poisoned while on a visit to the Tatars. After his father's death Temujin watched as most of his followers deserted to join other tribes where they could expect more protection than they could from the boy prince. Left almost entirely destitute, Temujin and his mother and brothers scratched out what existence they could on the steppe by hunting and fishing. An event happened at this time that illustrates Temujin's character. He squabbled with his half-brother Bekter over a fish that one of them had caught and Temujin and his brother Kasar later ambushed Bekter and shot him to death with bow and arrow. There may have been something of a dynastic character to this murder as illegitimacy was no bar to succession and Bekter was his elder; Temujin likely wanted no disputes over who was in authority, even in his reduced situation.

Temujin's fortunes had reached their lowest ebb when he was captured by the neighboring tribe of the Taijits. He was able to escape and began a slow process of attracting followers and finding a protector. He became the vassal of Toghrul, Khan of the Keraits (a Nestorian Christian who is probably the source of the persistent Prester John myths of Europe) and eventually went on to supplant him. Temujin fought and defeated the Merkits, the Naimans and the Tatars. It appears that he largely annihilated these latter people for their part in the death of his father, though the later tendency of Europeans to refer to Mongols as Tartars suggests that this may not be entirely correct; they might still have been numerous enough in the thirteenth century Mongol armies which ranged westward to give the confederation their name.

After many years of war he managed to gain supremacy over all of the steppe tribes of central Asia and took the title Jinghiz Khan. He became the "Khan of all who dwelt in felt tents" and, later, he styled himself "The Emperor of All Men".

Jinghiz Khan went on to conquer much of northern China, and to overthrow the wealthy and powerful state of Kwarizm, much of which lay in what is now Iraq. His army conducted a reconnaissance into Russia and Central Europe, and he undoubtedly wished to extend his conquests further into the west. His successes had convinced him at some point that he was divinely appointed to conquer the world. Fortunately for Europe neither he nor his successors did so. Nonetheless, when he lay dying in 1227 from internal injuries gotten in a fall from horseback while hunting, he was said to impart to his sons the task of conquering what remained since he was not to live long enough to do it himself. Carpini remarks on this mandate in the *Historia*.

Jinghiz Khan was succeeded by his son Ogedei who, when he became Great Khan, undertook to continue the work of conquest that his father had so successfully begun. The Mongol Empire had already been divided to a large degree among the sons of Jinghiz Khan. They were all to obey Ogedei as he was the Great Khan, but many of them ruled appanages spread over different parts of the steppe. Of these, the one of most consequence for Europe was that of Batu. Batu was Jinghiz Khan's grandson by his son Juchi, whose paternity was in some doubt. Jinghiz Khan's wife had been kidnapped shortly after their wedding and, until her rescue, had been given to the nobleman of another tribe. Juchi had been given an appanage to the west which had passed to his son Batu upon his death in 1227. Batu's holdings were not as large as the others, and Ogedei decided to mount a campaign into the west to expand them. The expedition was nominally in charge of the young Batu, but Ogedei had chosen as general Subotai, Jinghiz Khan's great commander. It was he who planned and conducted the campaign in the west.

The campaign was the strategic and tactical masterpiece discussed above. The result was the utter defeat of the western armies sent against them, the devastation and depopulation of Hungary, and a sense of shock and despair throughout the west which did not understand who the Mongols were or what they planned.

When the Mongols mysteriously disappeared into the Russian steppe the west convinced itself that the barbarian had been driven back by western arms and the cost of taking Hungary. This was untrue. Ogedei Khan had died three thousand miles away in the heart of Central Asia and the Mongol leaders had halted their campaign to go to Karakorum for the election of the new Khan. Apparently, from the Mongol standpoint, Europe could wait. It was a great piece of luck, for it turned out to be more than a reprieve. Batu Khan now controlled Russia through his own state, Golden Horde, and after the death of Ogedei the imperial *tumens*, or divisions of ten thousand soldiers, which had been lent for the western campaign were returned to Asia. Without them Batu may have felt that he did not have the power to hold Hungary. Instead, aside from a few raids, he satisfied himself with consolidating his hold on the Russian steppe where the Golden Horde would impose the "Tartar Yoke" upon the Russians for nearly two hundred years.

Discord between the various branches of the Golden Family (Jinghiz Khan's descendants) would gradually cause the Mongol Empire to break into several autonomous khanates such as the Golden Horde, the White Horde, the Great Horde, the Little Horde, the Ilkhanate and the Khanates of Astrakhan, Kazan and the Crimea. Even while the Mongol Empire was still nominally unified, however, its incipient divisions were enough to prevent the Mongols' return to Europe.

It might seem odd that a tribe of barbarians could, through conquest and assimilation of others like themselves, eventually invade and defeat powerful civilized nations such as China, Kwarizm, the Russian principalities, Hungary, and later, Persia. However, steppe peoples do have certain natural advantages which, when properly harnessed, could turn them into the most formidable of military powers. Their first quality is simply that of toughness. Living as they did on the steppe, often in semi arid regions, and forced to move from winter to summer pasturage twice a year, they became much more toughened than sedentary peoples. They often had to fight over grazing lands with other tribes when climactic or political changes made it necessary. In short, they were always in fighting trim. Edward Gibbon said it as well as anyone in his *Decline and Fall of the Roman Empire* when discussing steppe peoples:

> On this occasion, as well as on many others, the sober historian is forcibly awakened from a pleasing vision, and is compelled, with some reluctance, to confess that the pastoral manners, which have been adorned with the fairest attributes of peace and innocence, are much better adapted to the fierce and cruel habits of a military life.
>
> [Vol I, Chapter XXVI, p 901]

And further:

> The palaces of the rich consist of wooden huts, of such a size that they may be conveniently fixed on large waggons, and drawn by a team perhaps of twenty or thirty oxen. The flocks and herds, after grazing all day in the adjacent pastures, retire, on approach of night, within the protection of the

camp. The necessity of preventing the most mischievous confusion in such a perpetual concourse of men and animals must gradually introduce, in the distribution, the order, and the guard of the encampment, the rudiments of the military art. As soon as the forage of a certain district is consumed, the tribe, or rather army, of shepherds makes a regular march to some fresh pastures, and thus acquires, in the ordinary occupations of the pastoral life, the practical knowledge of one of the most important and difficult operations of war.

[Ibid, pp 903-904]

That "most important and difficult operation" which Gibbon refers to would be called "logistics" today, and it was something very poorly handled by the western armies of the dark and middle ages. Its importance cannot be overestimated; it could happen that medieval European armies might not even find each other when they wished to fight. The Mongols, by contrast, could break up their forces and have them operate independently hundreds of miles apart to achieve strategic objectives, something the west had not been able to do since the days of the Roman Empire. Less elegantly put, any tribe of steppe people were already, of necessity, a quasi-military organization in sharp distinction to settled peoples and this gave them a distinct advantage on campaign over townsmen until the discovery of gunpowder permanently shifted the balance in favor of settled peoples. Thus the Mongols presented a medieval reprise of the problem the Roman Empire had faced centuries earlier in the guise of the Huns. The Huns, however, had largely disappeared from history upon the death of their Khan, Attila; the Mongols did not. In this way more than in any other, the Mongols are distinguished from their Hunnish avatars.

The Mongols were much more successful than the Huns, and two reasons are clear: Jinghiz Khan, after the disillusionment of his youth when he saw his tribe melt away from him at his father's death, made a practice of attaching to himself men of other tribes whom he could trust. For example, many of his generals such as Subodei, Jebe and Jelme were none of them actually Mongols. Furthermore, when a hostile tribe was conquered, its fighters were dispersed into different *tumens,* or regiments, of the army so there was no core of dissidents anywhere to destabilize it. In short, Jinghiz Khan created an artificial tribe of the Mongols to whom the disparate members of allied, or broken tribes, would owe their loyalty. Thus, the Tartars whom Carpini met were more often Kipchak Turks, Naimans, Karakytai or Tartars rather than true Mongols by ethnic descent.

The instrument of the Mongol Empire was, of course, the army. As an army of horse archers it differed radically from the knightly armies of western Europe. A second major difference was one of organization, or more properly the difference is that they were organized. The Mongol army, unlike western armies of the period, was disciplined, and ordered according to a decimal system into units of ten, one hundred, one thousand, and ten thousand men. It hardly need be said that the western armies had no such organization. The knights would form into irregular "battles" of different size, composition and national or local origin. A group of these battles formed the line and the contest was joined. Nobles fought over precedence in the line of battle and command was assigned on the basis of birth, not, as in the Mongol armies, on the basis of proven competence.

The Mongol armies were made up entirely of cavalry, about two thirds of which were considered light cavalry and the rest heavy cavalry. However, even the more heavily equipped soldiers were much more lightly equipped than a knight. Furthermore, the Mongol horseman depended upon his bow and never closed with an adversary before he was beaten. His protection lay in speed and maneuverability, not in armor. The Mongol bow was a recurved, composite bow laminated of sinew, wood and horn. It could cast an arrow more than two hundred yards and the Mongols could shoot them with great accuracy while riding at a good clip; they could even shoot accurately backwards at a pursuer.

The Mongol rode a pony rather than the large war charger of the western armies. This animal was smaller and tougher and survived by grazing in the wild. Each Mongol soldier had two, three or even four ponies so that he could spell them on a march and save them from exhaustion. This allowed Mongol armies to travel fifty or even sixty miles in a day, several times the distance that a western army of the period could.

The Mongols used the age old tactics of the steppe: they would generally meet their enemies in a loose crescent formation with either flank prepared to envelope the enemy. Often the attack was followed by a false retreat to draw the enemy after them. As the enemy became disorganized during the pursuit the Mongols would turn about at a chosen spot and try to attack the enemy's extended column along its flanks.. Sometimes they would hide troops in ambush and draw the enemy past them. While doing any of these things the disciplined Mongols took their orders from signal flags or, at night, from colored lanterns.

Finally, the Mongols used a calculated campaign of terror when they went to war. If a city resisted them and was then taken, virtually all of the inhabitants might be systematically slaughtered with a handful allowed to escape to the next city to spread panic about the Mongol approach. This technique often allowed the Mongols to take a number of cities without a struggle and accelerated their successes. It also caused them to be held by the Europeans and Middle Easterners who fought them in great fear and has earned them a reputation for ferocity which lasts even today.

But there was, of course, more to the Mongols than their campaigning, and while Carpini's report would explain somewhat their successes, it would also illuminate the people. Carpini's *Historia* is unique in being the first account by a European of the life and manners of Asia. Carpini would not be alone in having made the journey; others would soon follow, but he was the first. The cleric William of Ruysbroek would visit the Mongol capital of Karakorum somewhat later, and the papal envoy Andrew of Longjumeau visited the Mongol middle east, the Ilkhanate of Persia. The famous Polos would travel into China a few years later where the Grand Khan Kubilai now ruled. Marco Polo's *Description of the World* sets out his experiences and has been popular ever since, while unfortunately Carpini's work has never enjoyed this popularity.

How accurate is Carpini's account? It is in fact quite accurate so far as he reports what he saw. When he reports what he was told, though he undoubtedly considered carefully what he ought to believe, he could go wrong. This was because he was a man of his time, a man of the middle ages who saw nothing improbable in monsters or unlikely tales. Thus, the reader will find passages of minute accuracy on such things as military matters, while he will also encounter the odd fantastic story of dog faced men or of Prester John's Indians attacking the Tartars with fire pumped out of horse-borne copper dummies. Carpini was willing to accept tales from others which were consistent with what was generally believed (or at least expected) from Asia. In a similar way he saw the Kytai or Chinese as being much like Christians and even recounts that they honored Christ. They did not, of course, but Carpini clearly recognized the Chinese as civilized, a point he might be reserved upon in judging the tent-dwelling Tartars. Because they were civilized, Carpini naturally saw in them many of the qualities which formed the ground of his own civilization, and the assumption would easily follow that they must be familiar with Christ. And even more, there were Christians among the Mongols hordes, not simply Orthodox Russians, but Asiatic Christians of the Nestorian sect which had been practically forgotten in the west. The Nestorians had centuries before left Byzantine territory to avoid persecution for their unorthodox beliefs and the west had nearly forgotten them.

Generally, therefore, when Carpini reports what he saw or experienced, the reader may be sure of its accuracy. The history of the rise of the Mongols, while garbled and larded with the odd tall tale, is correct enough in broad outline. After all, the Mongols themselves were illiterate during much of their rise to power and by Carpini's day, when they had begun to put down for themselves what had happened (and they did this very little, in any case) it was bound to be inexact and, retold through intermediaries to an outsider, details were bound to drop out, and wonders creep in. Carpini's geography was necessarily vague-- he could hardly have known where he was going or even quite how far-- except that it was a long way indeed. His description of Mongol warfare is most exact and, had the west decided to prepare for a conflict with them, it would have proved invaluable. Finally, Càrpini's account of his travels and of the election and enthronement of Guyuc Khan is unmatched. His account gives us a window on the medieval world and on the timeless experience of the traveller in a land both foreign and new.

Most probably as a reward for his efforts, Carpini was made Archbishop of Antivari in Dalmatia. The *Historia* is, unfortunately, his only surviving writing.

TRANSLATOR'S NOTE

This translation was prepared from a new edition of Carpini's *Historia* put out by the Centro Italiano Di Studi Sull'Alto Medioevo of Spoleto, edited by Enrico Menesto. This is a redaction of the various manuscripts in which the *Historia* is found. There are a number of abbreviated forms, and four longer manuscripts. Carpini himself mentions in chapter nine of his work that there were both long and short editions.

Carpini's work is relatively concise, but from the standpoint of style is not, strictly speaking, a literary work. In fact, Carpini was particularly fond of the passive voice, and of both long and short parenthetical statements which are often not too closely related to the main thrust of the sentence. He sometimes used both in the same sentence and this should be evident in the translation. Carpini placed his clauses in whatever order he saw fit, but even though English is more flexible than most modern languages and would allow an almost literal translation of these structures, they are almost unreadable from the standpoint of style. Besides, the interest of the text lies in what is said, not in how it is said. Therefore, I have taken the liberty, quite often, of reworking the order of the clauses for ease of reading, and I have recast a number of them in the active voice for the same reason.

Secondly, Carpini interspersed perhaps half of his sentences with words such as *enim* or *vero* which, while literally meaning "indeed" or "truly", were probably added for emphasis as medieval texts were commonly read aloud. The words themselves seldom add much to the sentence, and their repetition distracts from the narrative. I have therefore left them out where in English, they seem awkward. The same is true of certain other repetitive words which add little, if anything, to the meaning. *Predictus,* is an example. This means "the aforesaid" and Carpini uses the term freely after he has named someone. I believe the modern reader would rather not be troubled with "the aforesaid Chingis".

Carpini has the annoying tendency to use pronouns in referring to both Europeans and Tartars almost all of the time, and he very often does so in the same sentence. Thus, the text concerns various "theys" which must be sorted out by context. This is at best disconcerting and at worst confusing. I have therefore translated many of the "theys" and "thems" into the nouns for which they are the relative pronouns. Therefore, the words "Tartar" and "Tartars" often appear in place of the repetitive *qui* and *quos* for the sake of clarity and ease.

Obviously, part of the pleasure in reading an author from so long ago is to catch the flavor of the language, or as much as one can from a translation. I think that Carpini's style is so distinctive that it should be quite evident in this translation despite the concessions I have made toward a more colloquial translation. It is to keep the feeling of the text that I have left most of the names as they are in the text: Ierozlai for Yaroslav, Vasilco for Vasily, and such. Mongol names are often transcribed with astonishing variety today; I believe there are eleven ways of transliterating them. Mongol names have been kept as Carpini set them down: Bati instead of Batu, Occodei instead of Ogedei, Kuyuk instead of Guyuk, and so on. Most of them are clear enough, and the only exception is Chingis Khan for Chingiscan or Occodei Khan for Occodeican because this way both name and title are clear. The names of western or Russian cities or places are given as we would today: Kiev instead of Kiova, Kracow instead of Cracovia, Bohemia instead of Boemia, Bratislava instead of Wratislava. Similarly, I have kept Carpini's terms for the various peoples he met, hence, "Kytai" instead of Chinese, and "Comanus" instead of Kuman or Kipchak. In doing this I have kept to Latin plurals, because they seem to work with these words, except for names which we commonly use ourselves, hence "Saracens" instead of *Saraceni.*

For those interested in Carpini's Latin, it is typical. His vocabulary is fairly broad, but does contain non-classical words such as *barones* (barons) and *strepa* (stirrup) for the ranks of people and for objects that did not exist in classical times. He uses certain terms of rank very loosely, apparently meaning different things in different contexts. *Dux,* when he speaks of Europeans, generally means duke, or prince. When he speaks of the Mongols it seems to mean leader, or perhaps general. His use of *princeps* is somewhat unclear. In speaking of the Tartar leaders he often refers to them as *principes exercitum*. By this he probably does not mean "princes of the armies" but, more likely, generals. And yet *princeps* at other times applies to members of the Mongol royal family with its more obvious connotation of "prince".

Carpini's spelling shows the usual medieval tendencies to replace the dipthong "ae" with the simple "e" and the internal "h" with "ch" as, for example in "nichilominus" instead of "nihilominus". There is nothing particularly significant in this; it probably mirrors the pronunciation of the Latin he spoke. His grammar, meanwhile, suggests that of a modern Romance language; complex classical structures do not appear, or hardly appear. The famous *"ut"* clause of classical Latin is rare and then is only used where the subjunctive expresses uncertainty and where a modern Romance language such as Italian or French might use the subjunctive voice as well. Much more common are subordinate clauses introduced by *"quod"* (in the sense of "that") followed by an infinitive. This conforms to modern Romance usage.

PROLOGUE
Here Begins
the Story of the Mongols
Whom We Call the Tartars

To all who are faithful in Christ to whom this account may come, Brother John of Plan Carpini[1], of the Order of Friars Minor, Nuncio of the Apostolic See to the Tartars and other eastern nations wishes the grace of God now and the triumphant victory in the future of Our Lord Jesus Christ over the enemies of God.

When we learned the wish of the Lord Pope and the venerable cardinals and went to the Tartars and other eastern nations by order of the Holy See, we chose to set out to the Tartars first. We feared harm because of the Tartars' proximity to God's Church and so even though we feared death or permanent captivity by the Tartars or others, and though we feared hunger, thirst, cold, heat, injury and troubles beyond our strength, all of which happened to us many times and more than we would have believed earlier (except death and permanent captivity), we still did not dissuade ourselves from carrying out God's will according to the order of the Lord Pope, so that we might help the Christians, somewhat at least, to know the Tartars' attitude and intent, and so we can show this to the Christians lest, by appearing very suddenly the Tartars should discover them unprepared, as happened once before[2] through men's sins, and do a great massacre of the Christian people.

Therefore, we write this to you as a warning and you should freely believe it because we saw everything with our own eyes, since we walked a great deal among the Tartars for a year and four months and likewise lived among them or heard from Christians who are captives among them whom we believed worthy of trust. Indeed, we had a commission from the Most High Pope to carefully examine the whole and to see everything. We and Brother Benedict the Pole of the same order who shared our trials and was our companion and interpreter did this thoroughly.

However, if anything we write into the account of the embassy is unknown in your parts you must not for that reason call us liars, because we relate to you those things we ourselves saw or heard for certain from others whom we believe trustworthy. It is certainly a harsh thing when a man, because of the good he does, is reviled by others.

CHAPTER ONE

The Tartar Country, its Location and Description, and its Weather

B ecause we wish to write about the Tartars so that readers may learn about them easily, we shall describe them in chapters arranged this way: first we shall describe the country, second the people, third the religion, fourth the customs, fifth their empire, sixth their tactics, seventh the lands which they have conquered, eighth how to wage war against them, and finally the route which we took, the court of the emperor, and the districts of the empire and the witnesses who came upon us in the Tartar country.

We propose to treat the country this way: first, we shall describe its location, second, its nature, and third, its weather.

This country lies to the north east. To the east is the land of the Kytae[3] as well as the Solangi. To the south is the land of the Saracens[4] and between the west and south is the land of the Huyri[5], to the west of it is the province of the Naimans[6] and to the north the Ocean surrounds it.

This country is partly mountainous and partly plains, but as a rule it is a mixture of gravel and sand. In one part of the country are a good number of forests, while other parts have no wood. When the Tartars cook their food, even the emperor and the princes and all the others sit at a fire made of the dung of cattle and horses. The land is only in the hundredth part fruitful and cannot support crops unless irrigated, however water and streams there are few and the rivers rare. In their country there are no villages or cities, except one, substantial enough to be called a city, and that is named Caracoron[7]. We did not see it, although we were half a day from it when we visited the Syra Horde[8] which is the emperor's largest camp. And though the land is poor, it is not completely so, for it is good enough to support flocks.

The weather there is extremely variable. In fact, in the middle of summer, when other areas usually have the greatest heat, there is a good deal of thunder and lightning which kills many people, and a great deal of snow actually falls there then. There are great cold windstorms too, so that often men can ride horses only with difficulty. Therefore when we came to the horde (as their emperor's and princes' camps are called) we had to throw ourselves flat to the ground because of the force of the wind, and there was so much dust we could hardly see. In winter it never rains there, while in summer it often does, but so little that it can hardly soak the dust and roots of the pastures. Hail, by contrast, falls abundantly. Once, at the time chosen for the Emperor to be enthroned, we were at the court and so much hail fell that when it suddenly melted, we understand that more than one hundred and sixty people in the camp were drowned and many huts were swept away too. And in the summer there may suddenly be extreme heat and then suddenly extreme cold. During the winter in one area a very great deal of snow falls, while in another very little.

To conclude briefly about the country: it is very large, but even though we saw it ourselves because we wandered through it for five months and because we travelled across the middle of it, it is much poorer than we can say.

CHAPTER TWO

The People, their Clothes, Homes, Possessions and Marriages

Now that we have described the country we must describe the people. First we shall treat their persons, second their marriages, third their clothes, fourth their homes and fifth their possessions.

Their appearance is quite different from that of everyone else. Tartars have eyes and cheeks wider apart than other men. Their cheeks stick out a good deal from the jaw and they have a flat middle-sized nose and small eyes and eyelids raised to the eyebrows. They are generally narrow in the waist, except for a few, and almost all are of middling height. Few of them have much of a beard, though some have a small amount of hair on the upper lip and in the beard which they seldom trim. They cut the hair on the top of the head like a cleric, and generally everyone shaves from one ear to the other to a width of three inches by which cut of the crown the ears are joined. Everyone shaves above the forehead to the width of two inches in a similar way, however the hair which is between the crown and the shaved fringe they allow to grow to the eyebrows and because each side of the forehead is cut more than in the middle, they grow the middle hair long; the rest of the hair they let grow as women do and make two braids of it and tie each one behind the ear.[9] They have middle-size feet.

Everyone has as many wives as he can afford: some have a hundred, some fifty, some ten, some more, some fewer, and everyone is generally married to relatives except to their own mother or daughter or sister of their own mother-- even to half sisters and they can actually marry their father's wives after his death. In fact, the younger of two brothers may marry the elder brother's wife after his death or else another younger relative may do so. They take all the rest of the women as wives without any distinction and they buy them from their relatives at great cost. After the death of their husbands the women do not willingly marry a second time, unless someone wishes to marry his stepmother.

Their clothes, whether for men or women, are of one style: they do not wear cloaks, caps, hoods or stoles. Instead they wear tunics of buckram, fine fabric or silken fabric made in this way: from the top downwards they are cut open and they are folded double across the breast, and they are closed at the left side by one cord and on the right by three. On the left side it is cut open to the waist. All fur clothes are made in this way: the top fur garment has the hair outside, but is open at the back and has a tail at the back down to the knee.

Women who are married have a very full tunic right to the ground cut open down the front. They wear a round thing made of basketry or bark on the head which stands up a foot and a half and at the top spreads into four. From the base to the top it grows wider and at the top it has a long and graceful wand of gold, silver, wood or even feathers and it is sewed onto a cap which drapes down to the shoulders. And this cap, just like the outfit already described, is made either of buckram, felt or silk. Married women are never seen by men without this headdress, and by it they are known from the other women. Maidens, however, and other young women can be told from men only with great difficulty because they are dressed like the men. The Tartars have hats different from other peoples' whose form we cannot clearly describe.

Tartar homes are round and prepared like tents made cleverly of laths and sticks.[10] In the middle of the roof there is a round window through which light comes in and smoke can leave, because they always have a fire in the center. The walls and the roof are covered by felt and even the doors are made of felt. Some huts are large and some are small, depending upon the wealth or poverty of the owners. Some are taken apart quickly and put back together again and carried everywhere; some cannot be taken apart but are moved on carts. The smallest are put on a cart drawn by one ox, the larger by two or three or more depending upon how large it is and how many are needed to move it. Whenever they travel, whether to war or other places, they always take their homes with them.

The Tartars are quite rich in animals: camels, cattle, sheep, goats, and they have so many horses and mares that we did not believe there were that many in all the world, but they have few pigs or other animals.

The emperor, the dukes and the other nobles are wealthy and have gold, silver, silks, precious stones and gems.

CHAPTER THREE

Religion, What the Tartars Believe are Sins; Divination, Absolution and Funeral Rites

N ow that we have described the people, we will deal next with religion in this way: first we will discuss the Tartar religion, second, what they believe are sins, third, divination and the purging of sins and fourth, their funeral rites.

The Tartars believe in one God whom they think is the creator of all things visible and invisible, and they believe he gives rewards and punishments in this world.[11] Even so, they do not worship him with praises or ritual. Nevertheless they do have idols of felt made in the image of men and they place these on both sides of the doorway of a tent and underneath it the put a thing of felt made in the shape of an udder and they believe that these protect their flocks and are responsible for milk and offspring. In fact the Tartars make other idols of silk rags and honor these greatly. They place them in a beautiful roofed cart before the door of a hut and whoever steals anything from the cart is killed without mercy. When the Tartars wish to make idols, all of the important ladies in the camp convene and make them reverently and kill a sheep and eat it and burn its bones in a fire. And when a boy falls sick they make an idol in the same way and tie it above his bed. Generals, commanders of thousands and commanders of hundreds have a shrine in the middle of their camp.

The Tartars offer the first milk of all the flocks and herds to these idols, and when they begin to eat or drink they first make an offering to them from the cup or pot. And when the Tartars kill an animal they offer the heart to the idol in the cart in a shallow bowl and leave it until morning and then take it away from its presence and cook and eat it. The Tartars have made an idol of the first emperor which they have put in a cart in a place of honor before the horde of the current emperor, which we saw, and they offer many gifts to it. They offer horses to it, which no one dares ride as long as they live, and they offer other animals to it which they kill to eat but they do not break any of their bones; instead they burn them in a fire. Then they bow to the south, as though to God, and they make other nobles who submit do the same.

Because of this it happened recently that when Michael, one of the princes of Russia, came to submit to Bati, the Tartars first tried to make him pass between two fires. After this they said that he should bow south to Chingis Kahn, but he replied that he would gladly bow to Bati and his servants but not to the image of a dead man because this is improper for a Christian. When he was repeatedly told through his son Yaroslav that he must bow, and yet he refused, Bati ordered Prince Michael killed if he would not bow. The prince replied that he preferred to die rather than do what was wrong. Bati sent Michael to one of his followers who trampled on his chest with his boots until the prince died. Meanwhile the prince comforted one of his soldiers who stood near him by saying: "Be strong because your punishment will not last long and then at once eternal joy will follow." After this his head was cut off quickly with a knife.[12] The soldier, to tell the truth, also had his head cut off with a knife.

The Tartars worship only the sun and the moon and especially fire and water and they worship the earth, offering to them the first things from their cups and pots especially in the morning after which they eat and drink. Because they do not observe any law of the religion of God, they force no one, so we understand, to break their own faith or law, with the exception of Michael discussed above. We do not know what they do beyond this; it is assumed by some however, that if the Tartars had the power, and God turned away, they would make everyone bow to this idol.

While we were in the Tartar country Andrew, Prince of Chernigov (which is in Russia), appeared before Bati accused of having rustled Tartar horses and sold them elsewhere, and even though this was not proven he was killed. When his younger brother heard this, he came with the dead man's wife to Prince Bati to ask that his land not be taken from him. Bati told the boy that he should marry his own brother's wife and he told the woman she should take him as a husband in the Tartar manner. The prince replied that he would rather die than act against the law. But Bati nevertheless dragged her to him (though they struggled as much as they could) and the Tartars led them both to a bed and put the boy above the girl who screamed and cried, and forced them to have intercourse by extreme force.

Even though the Tartars have no law to do justice or prevent sin, all the same they do claim certain actions are sins which they or their ancestors have established. One of these is to thrust a knife into a fire or to touch fire in any way with a knife, or to pull meat from the flames with a knife, or to cut wood with a hatchet next to a fire. They actually believe that the head of the fire would be cut off in this way. Also, one must not lean on the whip with which one strikes a horse (they do not use spurs), or touch an arrow with a whip, or kill or catch young birds, or strike a horse with a bridle, or strike one bone with another, or toss milk or other drink or food on the ground. Also one must not urinate inside a tent.

If a person does this intentionally he is killed; if done otherwise he must pay a heavy fine to a sorcerer who purifies him and he must have the tent and all that is in it pass between two fires, but before it is purified this way no one dares enter or take anything from it. Also, if a piece of food is given to anyone and he cannot eat it and he spits it out of his mouth, a hole is made beneath the tent and he is drawn out through the hole and killed without mercy, and if anyone treads on the threshold of the tent of any prince he is killed this way. And they have many similar customs that are too numerous to recount.

However, to kill men, invade others' lands, acquire others' goods by unjust methods, to fornicate, to do injury to other men, to act against the commands received from God is not a sin among them.

They know nothing of eternal life or perpetual damnation. They believe, however, that after death they live in another world, that flocks multiply, that they shall eat and drink and do other things which living men do in this world.

The Tartars practice a great deal of divination, augury, magic, and incantations, and when demons respond they believe God himself is speaking to them. They call God "Utoga" (though the Comani[13] call him "Kam") -- and they fear and revere him and give many

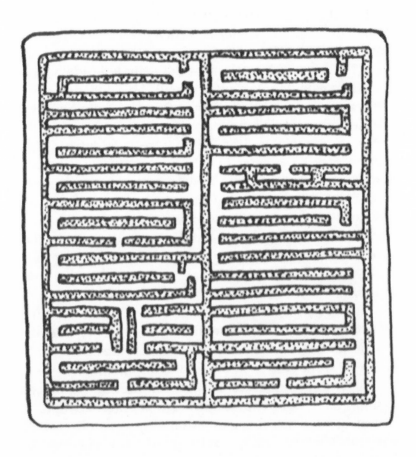

2. An Imperial Mongol Seal

offerings and the first drops from their cups according to their universal custom. Whatever new project they wish to begin, they start at the new moon or the full moon because they deem it a great power and kneel and pray to it. The Tartars say the sun is the mother of the moon because the moon receives light from it. And, briefly, they believe everything is purified through fire. Therefore, when ambassadors or foreign princes, or others, visit them, they and the baggage they carry must pass between two fires and be purified, lest perhaps they work a spell, or bring magic or some evil. Also, if a falling star passes in the sky over herds or men (which often happens there), or if some such thing should happen to them, which makes them believe they are defiled or unlucky, they must be purified in a similar manner by the incantations of sorcerers. They place almost all their faith in such things.

When one of them sickens to the point of death, a spear is put there and black felt is wound around it, and from then on no outsider dares enter the boundaries of this camp. When he begins to die almost everyone draws away from him because no one who attends his death can enter the horde of any leader or emperor until the new moon.

When one of them dies, if he is a noble, he is buried secretly in a field that pleases them. What is more, he is buried sitting in the middle of one of his tents, and they place a table before him and put a tray of meat and a bowl of mare's milk on it. Furthermore, there is buried with him a mare with a foal and a horse with a saddle and bridle, and they eat another horse and fill the skin with straw and mount it on two or four poles up high, so that in the next world he may have a tent where he may stay, and a mare from which he may have milk and by which he may increase the number of his horses and the horses he may ride. They burn for his spirit the bones of the horse they ate, and often women come to burn bones for the spirits of men as we saw with our own eyes, and others told us the same thing. Indeed, we saw the bush that Ogodei Khan, the father of the current emperor, ordered to be grown for his soul. The Tartars teach that no one may go there, and whoever takes a twig from there, as we saw, is beaten, stripped and badly treated. And when we really needed some switches to strike our horses with we did not dare take any from there. The Tartars bury gold and silver with him; the cart in which he was drawn is broken, and no one dares name anyone with his name until the third generation.

There is another way the Tartars bury some great men. They go secretly into a field and dig up a plant with its roots and they make a large hole in the side of this pit underground, and they put a slave they have chosen beneath him; he lies there long enough that he begins to die, then they take him out so that he can breathe, and they do this three times, and if he survives he is thenceforward free and does whatever he wishes and is important in the camp and among his relatives. The dead man, however, is buried in the hole in the side of the pit with the things described above. The Tartars fill in the pit which is before his hole and put the shrub above it as it was before so that it may not be told from any other place.[14] They do otherwise as described above, but leave his tent outside in a field.

In the Tartar country there are two cemeteries, one in which emperors, princes and all the nobles are buried, and no matter where they die, if possible, they are brought there. There is in fact a great deal of gold and silver buried with them. The other cemetery is the one in which the men who were killed in Hungary are buried, for many were killed there. No one dares approach this cemetery except the guards who are posted there to watch. If anyone does enter he is taken, stripped, beaten, and very badly treated. Indeed we ourselves unknowingly entered the boundaries of the cemetery of those killed in Hungary and the guards came upon us and wanted to shoot us with arrows, but because we were ambassadors and did not know the customs of the country they let us go.

Relatives and anyone else who remained in the hut must be purified through fire. The purification is done this way: they build two fires and they place two spears near the fires and a line between the tips of the spears and they tie onto the line strips of buckram beneath which and between the two fires the people, animals and tents pass. There are two women, one here and the other there who throw water and recite certain songs, and if somehow the cart is broken there, or something should fall the sorcerers keep it. And if someone is killed by lightning all the people who lived in the household must pass between the fires in the aforesaid way; tent, bed, cart, felt and clothes and whatever things of that kind he possessed are not touched by anyone, but are treated by everyone just as if they were defiled.

CHAPTER FOUR

Their Good and Bad Customs,
their Food and their Habits

Now that we have spoken about their religion we must tell about their customs which we shall treat this way: first we shall tell what is good about the Tartars, second what is bad, third what their food is and fourth their habits.

The aforesaid men (namely the Tartars) obey their lords more than anyone else in the world, whether clergymen or laymen, and they respect them greatly and do not easily lie to them. The Tartars seldom argue to the point of insult, and there are no wars, quarrels, injuries or murders among them. In fact, there are no robbers and thieves of valuables there, so that the camps and carts where they keep their treasures are not protected by locks or bars. If animals become lost, whoever finds them leaves them or sends them to men who are commissioned for this; the owners ask for them and receive them with no difficulty. Each man respects his fellow and they are friendly to each other, and though food is scarce among them, still there is enough to share. Their life is so hard that when they fast for a day or two and eat nothing they do not seem unhappy, but sing and play just as though they ate well. When riding horses they tolerate great cold and heat. Nor are the men touchy; they do not appear jealous of their neighbors, and it seems that none are envious. No man turns another away, but instead helps him and supports him as much as possible.

Their women are chaste, and one never hears scandals about them, though they tell coarse and vulgar jokes. The women seldom or never have affairs. Sometimes they become quite drunk, yet while drunk they never fight with words or blows.

Now that we have described the Tartars' good points, we must to set down the bad. The Tartars are prouder than other men and despise everyone else; indeed it is as though they held outsiders for nothing whether noble or base born.

In fact, at the court of the emperor we saw the nobleman Ierozlai[15], Great Duke of Russia, the son of the King and Queen of Georgia, many great sultans, and even the Emir of the Solangi fail to receive the honors due them, but instead the Tartars who were assigned to them were very rude, walked in front of them and always took the first and highest place; in fact these nobles always had to sit behind them.

The Tartars become quite angry with other men, are indignant by nature and lie to all outsiders: almost no truth is found among them. At first they are very mild, but in the end they sting like a scorpion. The Tartars are subtle and treacherous and, if they can, they get around everything by cunning. The men are filthy with regard to their clothing, food and other things, and whatever evil they wish to do to others they hide amazingly well so that the victims cannot protect themselves or find a solution to their cunning. Drunkenness is honorable among the Tartars, and when someone drinks a great deal he is sick right on the spot, and this does not prevent him from drinking more. They are very jealous and greedy, demanding of favors, tenacious of

what they have and stingy givers, and they think nothing
of killing foreigners. In short, because their evil habits
are so numerous they can hardly be set down.

They regard anything which can be eaten as food:
they eat dogs, wolves, foxes and horses, and, when in
difficulty, they eat human flesh.[16] Thus, when they
attacked a particular Chinese city, and their emperor
himself conducted the siege, they found after they had
besieged it a long while that the Tartars had used up all
their supplies and did not have enough for all the men
to eat, so they took one of every ten men to eat. They
even eat the afterbirth which comes out of a mare with
the foal. Furthermore, we saw them eat lice. They
would say, "Why should I not eat them when they eat
my children and drink their blood?" We actually saw
them eat mice.

The Tartars do not use tables or napkins. They do
not have bread, oil, vegetables, or anything else besides
meat, and they eat so little of this that other people
could hardly live on it. When they dirty their hands a
great deal with meat grease as they eat, they wipe their
hands upon their shins, or upon leaves or something of
that kind. It is true, however, that the more noble
usually have little rags with which, at the end, they clean
their hands when they eat meat. One of them cuts and
the other takes morsels with the point of a knife and a
Tartar offers either more or less meat to another
depending upon whether he wishes to honor him less or
more. They do not wash their bowls, but sometimes
rinse them with broth and replace the broth again with
the meat in a jar. If they clean them, they wash jars or
spoons or other vessels used for this in a similar way. It
is a great sin among them if any food or drink is allowed
in any way to go to waste; they are not permitted to give

bones to dogs unless the marrow is first extracted. The Tartars do not wash their clothes, or permit them to be washed, especially when there is thunder, until it ends. They drink mare's milk in great amounts. If they should happen to have it, they drink the milk of sheep and cows, goats and even camels. The Tartars do not have wine, ale, or mead unless it is sent by other people or given to them. In winter, unless they are rich, they do not have mare's milk. They cook millet with water, which they make so thin that they can drink rather than eat it. And each one of them drinks one or two cups in the morning, and then nothing more during the day. In the evening however each is given a very small amount of meat, and drinks meat broth. In summer because they have enough mare's milk, they rarely eat meat unless it happens to be given to them or they take some animal or bird by hunting.

By law or custom they kill men and women whom they discover in open adultery. It is the same with a virgin: if she has been slept with they kill the man and the woman. If someone is caught openly robbing or stealing in their domain he is killed without mercy. If one of them reveals their plans, especially when they wish to go to war, he is given a hundred strokes on the back mostly with a so stick so heavy it would take a peasant to handle it. Also, when one gives slight offense in something the Tartars do not spare him because of his rank but beat him severely with switches. There is no difference between the son of a concubine and a wife and a father can give whatever he wishes to either one. If the son is descended of a noble then the son of the concubine is just as noble as the son of the legitimate wife. When a Tartar has many wives (according to his station and family), he eats and drinks and sleeps with one on one day and the others on other days. However, one of them is foremost among them and he stays with her more than with the others, and even when there are many of them they do not fight among themselves.

The men do no work except archery, though sometimes they take care of the herds. Instead they hunt and work at shooting. All of them from the children to the adults are good archers, and their children, when they are two or three years old, begin to ride. They ride and gallop, and bows are given to the children according to their size and they are taught to shoot; they are very apt and daring besides.

Girls and women ride and gallop on horses as skillfully as men. We even saw them carrying quivers and bows, and the women can ride horses for as long as the men; they have shorter stirrups, handle horses very well, and mind all the property. The Tartar women make everything: skin clothes, shoes, leggings, and everything made of leather. They drive carts and repair them, they load camels, and are quick and vigorous in all their tasks. They all wear trousers, and some of them shoot just like men.

CHAPTER FIVE

The Founder of the Tartar Empire, its Princes and the Power of the Emperor and his Government

N ow that we have spoken of their customs, their domain must come next. First we shall tell of their state, second of their leaders and third of the power and government of the emperor and his state.

There is a certain land of the Tartars in the east, which we have mentioned above, called "Mongal". At one time this land had four people: one was the Yeka Mongol[17], that is, the so-called Great Mongols; the second was the Sumongal, that is, the Water Mongols. These, however, called themselves Tartars[18] from a river that runs through their land called "Tartar". Another was a people called the Merkit, and the fourth was the Mecrit[19]. All these peoples were of the same race and language, but were divided among themselves by territories and princes.

There was a man in the Yeka Mongol country called Chingis[20]. He started as a great hunter by the grace of God. Chingis incited men to steal and plunder and went into foreign lands and whomever he could take and associate with himself he would not dismiss. Therefore, he recruited men of his own race and they followed him as their leader to commit any crime. Chingis began to fight with the Sumongals or Tartars after which they convened and killed their leader, and after a great deal

3. Chinese portrait of Chingis Khan

of war he defeated the Tartars and forced them into servitude. After this Chingis fought with all of these peoples: with the Merkits (who were located next to the Tartar land) and he subjected them to himself by war; After this he proceeded to fight the Mecrits and defeated them too.

When the Naimans heard that Chingis had become so powerful they became angry. They had a state which was quite strong and all of the aforesaid people had given them tribute. When their leaders had died of old age, their sons succeeded to their place, but were young and stupid and did not know how to hold their people.

Instead the Naimans became divided or cut apart from one another, while at this same time Chingis was very powerful. Nevertheless the Naimans provoked Chingis in the lands described above and they killed his men and women and children and took their goods.

Chingis heard this and gathered all his subjects to him. The Naimans and the Karakytai (that is, the Black Kytai)[21] likewise gathered against him in a valley between two mountains (which we travelled through on the way to their emperor), and a battle was joined in which the Mongols defeated the Naimans and Karakytai. Most of them were killed and the others who could not escape were reduced to servitude.

Occodai Khan, the son of Chingis Khan, built a city after he was enthroned as emperor, in the country of these Karakytai and he called it Emil. It is near a great wasteland where it is said that forest people live who are mute and do not have knees,[22] so that if they fall they cannot get up without the help of others. But they have such skill that they make felt from the wool of camels by which they are clothed and which they use for tents. Whenever the Tartars attack them and wound them with arrows, they put grass in the wound and flee quickly from them.

The Mongols, then, returned to their own country, and prepared themselves for battle against the Kytai and, moving their camps, they invaded the Kytai country. However the emperor of the Kytai heard this and brought his army against the Tartars. A hard battle was joined in which the Mongols were defeated and all but seven of the Mongol nobles who were with this army were killed. So, whenever anyone threatens the Tartars by saying, "You will be killed if you attack this country, because a great number of valiant warriors have died here," they reply, "Once we were killed and only seven remained but all the same we have grown into a multitude, so we do not fear such things."

Chingis and the others who had survived fled to their own country and when the aforesaid Chingis had rested he prepared himself for battle once again against the Huyri and went off to war. The Huyri are Christians[23] of the Nestorian sect whom he defeated in war and the Tartars took up their script, for before this they had had no writing. Now, however, this script is called the Mongol script. From there Chingis advanced against the Sarruyurs and against the Karanitae and against the Voyrats and against the Cananae and he conquered all these nations.

At this point Chingis returned to his own country, and when things had quieted somewhat he had called all of his men together, and went back to war against the Kytai, and after a long fight, they took over a great part of the Kytai land. The Tartars had blockaded the Kytai emperor in his biggest city and besieged him for such a long time that the Tartar army weakened from the effort and did not have enough to eat so he, Chingis Khan ordered that they should give up one out of ten men to be eaten.[24] The Kytai in the city, meanwhile, fought bravely against the Tartars with engines and arrows and when they ran out of stones they threw melted silver in place of stones for the city was very rich. Now, when the Tartars had fought a long while but could not vanquish the Kytai through fighting, they dug a great tunnel under the earth from the camp to the middle of the city and dashed into the middle of the city and fought with the townsmen while those who were outside fought thusly: they beat down the city gates, entered the city and killed the emperor and many men, and they took the city and carried away the gold, silver and all the riches. When they had put their own men in charge of the Kytai country the Tartars went back to their own country. Then, immediately upon the defeat of the Kytai emperor, Chingis Khan was made emperor. However part of the Kytai lands, because they are in the sea, even to this day they have not taken.

The Kytai, whom we have discussed above, are pagans who have their own script and a new and old testament and lives of the fathers and hermits and buildings built like churches in which they pray at their own times, and say they have saints. They worship one god, honor Jesus Christ, and believe in eternal life, but they are not baptized. The Kytai honor and revere our scripture, approve of Christians and give them many alms. They seem to be good and humane. They do not have beards and the disposition of their face is much like that of the Mongols, but not so broad in the face. They have their own language. There are no better craftsmen to be found in the world in those trades in which people should stay skilled. Their country is very rich in grain, wine, gold, silver and silk and in all things necessary to sustain human life.

When things had quieted a bit Chingis Khan divided his army. One of his sons, named Tossu (also called "khan" which means "emperor"), he sent with the army against the Kumani whom he defeated after much fighting. After he defeated them Tossu returned to his own country.

He sent another son with an army against the Indians and he defeated Lesser India. The Lesser Indians are black Saracens called Ethiopians. Then the Tartar army advanced to battle against the Christians who live in Greater India. When he heard this, the king of that country, who is commonly called Bishop John[25], met him with all his army. He made copper dummies of men, put them on horseback with fire inside them, and a man behind with bellows. The Indians advanced against the Tartars with many such dummies and prepared horses and when they had come to the battle-ground they placed these horses next to one to another.

The men who were behind put I do not know what on the fire which was in these figures and pumped hard with the bellows. Because of this the enemy's men and horses were burned by Greek fire[26] and the air was polluted with smoke, and then the Indians shot arrows at the Tartars and wounded and killed many and they drove them in confusion from their borders. We have not heard that the Tartars ever went back.

As the Tartars returned through the wastes they came to a land where they discovered monsters in a female shape-- so we were told in all seriousness at the court of the emperor by Ruthenian[27] clerics and others who had spent a long time among the Tartars. When the Tartars asked them through numerous interpreters where the men of the country were, they answered that in that land whoever was born female had a human form, while the males had a dog's shape. When the Tartars prolonged their stay in this country, dogs in another part of a river gathered in one place, and even though it was a very cold winter they all threw themselves into the water. After this they rolled uncontrollably in the dust so that the dust mixed with the water and froze onto them. They would do this repeatedly so the ice formed over them densely and then they attacked the Tartars fiercely. When the Tartars shot arrows at them it was as if they shot against rocks: the arrows rebounded and in fact their other weapons could do them no damage either. The dogs however did the Tartars great harm and injured and killed many with bites and thus drove them from their borders, and because of this there is a saying among them: "Your father or brother was killed by a dog." Indeed those of their women whom they captured the Tartars took back to their own country and they were there until they died.

Then the Mongol army returned and came to the Burithabets' country which they conquered. The Burithabets are pagans and who have the most miserable of customs because when someone's father passes away they all gather around their relative and eat him; we were assured that this was true. These people do not have beards; indeed they carry certain piece of iron in hand, as we saw, with which they always pluck out the beard so thoroughly that if by chance any hairs grow in it they are quite misshapen. From there the army returned to its own country.

At the time that Chingis Khan divided his other armies, he himself went with a force to the east through the land of the Kirghiz, whom he did not defeat in the war and he went as far as the Caspian Mountains. These mountains, however, in the area where they approached are of adamantine stone and so attracted their arrows and iron weapons. It is thought that the people who lived among the Caspian Mountains heard the noise of the army and began to shatter a mountain. When the Tartars returned another time ten years later they found the mountain shattered. But when the Tartars tried to approach they could not do so because there was a cloud before them that they could not pass through because all who entered it were immediately blinded. However, the mountain people believed that the Tartars planned to approach them and so they attacked them, but when they came to the cloud they could go no further for the same reason. The Tartars had travelled more than a month through a vast waste-land before they came to these mountains.

From there to the east, the Tartars travelled for more than a month through a great wasteland to a certain country (so we were assured), where they saw three roads, though they could not find a single person. Still, the Tartars searched the land so thoroughly that they found a single man and his wife whom they led before Chingis Khan. And when he had asked them where the people of that country were, they replied that they lived underground beneath mountains. So Chingis Khan kept the wife and sent the man to command these people to come as he ordered. This man in fact went to them and told them everything that Chingis Khan had ordered. They replied that they would come to Chingis Khan on a particular day to do his bidding. Meanwhile these men gathered by ways hidden beneath the earth and came against the Tartars to do battle and sprang suddenly upon them and killed many. So Chingis Khan and his men, seeing that the Tartars did not prevail at all, but rather lost men, and because they could not tolerate the sound of the sun (for at this time when the sun rises they must put one ear to the ground and stop up the other strongly lest they hear the terrible sound which, unless they are careful, would kill many of them) they fled the country. Chingis Khan took away these people, that is, the man and his wife, and he kept them in the Tartar country until their deaths. When they were asked why they lived beneath the earth, they said that once a year, when the sun rose, there was so much noise that men became senseless, as said of the Tartars above. In fact the people would play on organs and drums and other instruments at that time so they would not hear the sound.

As Chingis Khan and his men returned to their land they went through their provisions and were starving. It happened they found the fresh guts of an animal which they took and, removing only the dung, they cooked them and brought them out to Chingis Khan who ate them with his men. From this came Chingis Khan's law neither the blood, nor the intestines nor any other part of an animal which may be eaten shall be thrown away except the dung.

When he had returned to his own country Chingis Khan enacted many statutes and laws which the Tartars invariably observe, of which we relate only two. One is that whoever is so proud that by his own authority he claims the throne without election by the princes, he is to be killed without mercy. Because of this law one of the princes, a nephew of Chingis Khan, was killed, before the election of Cuyuc-- he had wished to reign without election. The other statute is that the Tartars must subject the entire world to themselves and have no peace with anyone unless they submit to the Tartars no matter how long it would take to kill them.

The Tartars have fought forty-two years and shall reign another eighteen years; after which they say that they must be defeated by another people-- they do not know who it might be; so it is prophesied among them. It is said that those who would escape the Tartars should follow the rules which those people obey who have defeated the Tartars in war. Their army must be organized by captains of thousands, captains of hundreds and captains of tens and common soldiers, thus groups of ten thousand men. There are many other statutes which take too long to tell, and indeed we do not know them. After his statutes and ordinances had been enacted Chingis Khan was killed by lightning.

Chingis Khan had four sons: Occodai, Tossu Khan, Chiaadai and we do not know the name of the fourth[28]. All of the Mongol princes descend from these four. First, of course was Occodai Khan, who had these sons: Cuyuc who now is emperor, Cocten and Sirenen. If he had other sons we do not know. These are the sons of Tossu Khan: Bati, who is the richest and most powerful after the emperor, Ordu, who is the eldest of all the princes, Siban, Bora, Berca, and Tanuht. We do not know the names of Tossu Khan's the other sons. The sons of Chiaadai are Burin and Cadan.[29] We do not know his other sons' names. There is another son of Chingis Khan whose name we do not know. The names of the sons are these: one is called Mengu whose mother is Seroctan; this lady is higher and more powerful among all the Tartars than any except the emperor's mother and Bati. Another is called Bechac. He has many sons, but we do not know their names.

Here are the names of their military leaders: Ordu, who was in Poland and Hungary; Bati, Burin, Cadan, Siban, and Buyget who were all in Hungary, and Chirpodan who went beyond the sea against the sultan of Damascus and others who are there. These others remain in their country: Mengu, Cocten, Sirenen, Hubilai[30], Sirenum, Sinocur, Thuatemyr, Coragai, Old Sibidei[31] (who is known as the great soldier among them) Bora, Berca, Moucy, and Choranca (but he is the least among them). Really, they have many leaders but we do not know their names.

The emperor of the Tartars has wonderful power over everyone. No one dares camp anywhere unless the emperor himself assigns the place. He himself assigns where the generals stay, the generals assign the millenarii their place, the millenarii assign the centenarii their place, and the centenarii the decani their place.[32] Furthermore, no matter what may happen to them, or what the time or place, whether or not in battle, even if it is a matter of life and death, they obey without argument. And if the emperor wishes their virgin daughter or sister, they give her to him without complaint. In fact, during one particular year or period he gathered virgins of a certain age from all the ends of Tartary and he kept the ones he wished and gave the others to his men as seemed useful to him.

The Emperor sends whomever he wishes as a messenger, and he sends as many of them as he wishes wherever he wishes. One must give these messengers the horses and expenses they commandeer without delay. No matter why they come, whether as tribute bearers or messengers one must likewise give them horses, carts and money.[33] However, ambassadors from other countries have little food or clothing because their allowances are mean and poor, especially when they visit the Tartar princes and have to extend their stay. What the Tartars give to ten men could hardly support two, and nothing is given to them at the court of the princes or on the road except once a day, and then hardly enough. Beyond this, if they have any troubles they can hardly deal with them, and so they must put up with them patiently. Furthermore, princes and other nobles and lesser men seek gifts from them, and if they do not give them the Tartars insult the ambassadors as though they were unimportant, and if the ambassador is sent by a great man they do not wish to take a small gift from him but say, "You come from a great man and give so little?" So the Tartars scorn to accept the gift, and if an ambassador really wishes to accomplish his task he must give them better. Roughly the largest part of the goods which were given to us by the faithful were given away because we had to make gifts of them.

And this must be known: it is as though everything belonged to the emperor, therefore no one dares say "This is mine or his," but rather everything belongs to the emperor whether things, men or horses, and he has recently enacted a statute about this. Similarly the generals have power over everything concerning their men. In fact, the men are divided, Tartars and everyone else, among the generals. Everyone (whether they are the emperor's men or someone else's) must give horses, expenses and men to a general's messengers, as well as men to take care of the horses and serve these messengers. The princes and others keep the horses of the emperor by twos and threes as he decides, but must give them back, so that he may have milk from them throughout the year. The generals' men are held to act for their lord and among them none is free. To put it briefly, whatever the emperor and the generals want they take of their men's substance; they dispose of their people in every way as it pleases them.

At the death of the emperor, as discussed above, the princes convened and elected Occodai, Chingis Khan's son, to the imperial office. He, by the usual custom of the princes, divided his army. He sent Bati, who had attained the second rank, against Altisoldan[34] and against the land of the Bisermini. These Bisermini were Saracens but spoke Coman[35]. He fought them and conquered. However, a certain city called Barchin resisted him a long while. The Bisermini had dug many holes around the city and worked very hard on them, so when the Tartars came to the city they fell into the holes and were unable to take this city before they had filled them in.

However, the men of a certain city called Ianikint heard this and went out to meet the Tartars and freely surrendered themselves so their city was not destroyed, though many of them they killed and others taken away. When the Tartars had taken the spoils of the city they settled it with other men and proceeded against the city of Ornas. This city was very populous: indeed there were many Christians there, Gazani, and Ruthenians and Alans and as well as Saracens, though the city government, was Saracen. Moreover, this city was full of riches and was located on a river which runs through Ianikint and the land of the Bisermini and enters the sea. So the city is almost a port and had the largest market of all the Saracen cities. When the Tartars could not defeat them any other way, they dammed up the river which ran through the city and submerged it with its goods and citizens. When they had done this, they then invaded the land of the Turks, who are pagans.

When these people had been defeated the Tartars advanced against Russia and devastated it.[36] They destroyed cities and castles and killed men and besieged Kiev, which is the greatest Russian city, and after a long siege they took Kiev and killed the townspeople, so when we went through that country we found countless human skulls and bones from the dead scattered over the field. Indeed Kiev had been a very great and populous city but now is reduced to almost nothing. In fact, there are hardly two hundred houses there now and the people are held in the strictest servitude. Carrying the war from there, the Tartars destroyed all of Russia.

The above-named generals then advanced from Russia and Comania and fought the Hungarians and Poles who killed many Tartars in Poland and Hungary. If the Tartars had not fled, the Hungarians would have driven the Tartars out of the country because they fought so hard and because the Tartars were so afraid and tried to flee. However Bati, unsheathed his sword and stood firm before the Tartars saying "Do not flee because, if you flee, none shall escape, and if we must die let us all die, that is what Chingis Khan predicted, but if there is still time, let us prevail." And so the Tartars were stirred and stood fast and destroyed Hungary.[37]

Returning from there they came into the land of the Mordvani who are pagans and conquered them. They proceeded from there against the Belorus, that is, Greater Bulgaria[38], and they destroyed it utterly. From there they went north against Bascart, that is, Greater Hungary, and defeated it too.

The Tartars left and went further north and came to the Parossitai who have small stomachs and mouths, so we would say that they do not eat, but instead cook meat which they place in a pot and breathe the fumes of and they are sustained by this alone. If they do eat anything it is very little.

Proceeding thence they came to the Samogedi. It is said that these people live only from hunting; the tents and clothes they have are only made of the skins of animals. Going further the Tartars came to a certain land beyond the ocean where they found monsters, as was forcefully told to us, that had in every way a human shape, but their feet ended in cattle feet and they have a human head but they have a face like a dog. They speak two words like a human being and the third they bark like a dog and so, over time they intersperse barks and yet come back to their nature and so what they say can be understood. From there the Tartars returned to Comania and some of them remain there yet.

At this time Occodai sent Chiropodan with an army south against the Kirghiz whom he conquered. These men are pagans who do not have hairy beards and whose custom is that when one's father dies, on account of sadness, they take off a strip of the face from ear to ear in sign of mourning.

When Chiropodan had defeated these people he went south against the Armenians. But as the Tartars crossed a wasteland they discovered certain monsters (as was told to us for certain), who had only one arm and hand in the middle of the chest and one foot and so that two of them shot as one person with a single bow, and they ran so fast that horses could not catch them. They ran jumping on this one foot and when they tired of going that way they would go on hand and foot revolving as in a circle. Isidore[39] called these people ciclopedes. And when tired they would run according to the earlier method. The Tartars killed a few of these people, as we were informed at the imperial court by a Ruthenian cleric, and when the above-named emperor died, many came as ambassadors in a legation to the emperor's court, already described above, so that they might have peace with him. The Tartars went from there to Armenia which they conquered as well as part of Georgia and they came to other parts according to their orders. The Armenians sent forty thousand *yperperum*[40] in a single year as tribute and still do.

From there the Tartars went to the land of the Sultan of Urum[41], who was great and powerful, and fought and conquered him. They proceeded further, fighting and conquering, up to the land of the Sultan of Damascus, and now they have taken that land and propose to fight other countries beyond these; from then until now they have not returned to their own country. Another army went against the land of the Caliph of Baghdad whom they subdued and whose people pay four hundred bezants a day besides silken fabric and other goods which he gives as tribute. And every year, on behalf of the Caliph, the people send ambassadors to the Tartars with wonderful gifts as tribute asking that they support them. The emperor himself accepts the gifts but nevertheless orders the Caliph to come to him.

CHAPTER SIX

War, the Organization of the Tartar Forces, their Arms, their Tactics when Fighting and their Cruelty to Captives, How they Besiege Forts, and their Treachery toward those who Surrender to them

N ow that we have discussed the empire we shall describe Tartar warfare in this order: first the organization of their army, second their arms, third their tactics, fourth the cruelty they exercise toward captives, fifth their investment of camps and cities, and sixth the treachery which they employ against those who surrender to them.

Chingis Khan organized the army this way: one man is set over ten and I call him a "decanus", one man is placed over ten decani whom I call a "centenarius", one man is placed over ten centenarii whom I call a "millenarius"[42], one man is placed over ten millenarii and they call this rank "darkness"[43]. Two or three generals are placed over the entire army but one is supreme.

When the line goes into battle, if one or two or three or more flee from the squad of ten, all ten are killed; and if all ten flee, unless the rest of the hundred flee, all of them are killed. Briefly, unless they give way together, all who flee are killed. Also, if one or two or more proceed daringly into the fight and the remainder of the ten do not follow, they are killed; and if one or more of the ten is captured and the other comrades do not free them, again they are killed.[44]

Everyone must have at least these weapons: two or three bows or at least one good one,[45] and three large quivers filled with arrows, a battle-axe and ropes for dragging machines. The rich, however, have swords which are sharp at the tip and honed on only one edge and somewhat curved, and they have horse armor, leg armor and a helmet and cuirass. Their cuirasses and horse armors are of leather and made this way: they take strips of cowhide or other animal hide of one hand's width wide, and they glue three or four or these together and tie them to each other with laces or cords. In the top strip they put the cords at the edge, in the one below they put them in the center and they do this until the end. Therefore, when the soldiers bend, the lower strips slide up over the upper ones and so they are doubled or even tripled over the body.

The Tartars make horse armor in five parts: they put one piece along each side of the horse which protects it from the tail to the head and is tied to the saddle, behind the saddle on the back, and at the neck. Over the horse's back they put another piece where the two parts of the harness are joined and they make a hole in this piece through which they expose the tail, while in front of the chest they place a piece that protects everything from the knees or the knee joints. On the forehead they put an iron plate which is tied on each side of the neck.

Their cuirass has four parts: one extends from the thigh to the neck but is made according to the shape of the human body; it is fitted to the front of the chest and from the arms on down it goes around the body. At the back they have another piece which extends from the neck down to the other piece which encircles the body; above the shoulders these two pieces (the front and the back) are joined by clips to two iron plaques on either shoulder; and on each arm they have a piece of armor. The part that extends from the shoulder down to the hand is open underneath at the lower part, and on each leg they have a piece of armor and all these are joined by clips.

The Tartar helmet has a crown made of iron or steel, but the part that extends around the neck and throat is of leather; and all these pieces of leather are made as described above.

Some Tartars, as we said above, have iron armor, and it is made this way: they make a number of thin plates as wide as a finger and as long as a palm, and they put eight little holes in each plate while underneath they lay tight and strong laces. They place the plates one over the other so they overlap, and then they tie these plates onto the strips with the slender laces which they put through the holes described above, and in the upper part they sew them to one lace so that the plates hold together well and firmly, and then they make something like a band of these plates, and then they tie them into sections described above, and they make horse armors as well as men's armor thusly, and they polish them until they shine so that a man can see his face in them.[46]

Some Tartars have lances with a hook at the head with which they drag men from the saddle if they can. The length of Tartar arrows is two feet and one palm and two fingers, and because feet vary we give a geometrical measure of the foot: two grains of barley make an inch and sixteen inches make a geometrical foot. Their arrowheads are very sharp and are honed on both sides like a two-edged sword. These arrowheads have a sharp haft a finger long which they embed in the shaft.[47]

The Tartars have shields of osiers or wicker but we do not believe they carry them except in camp while guarding the emperor or the princes and even then only at night. They have other arrows for shooting birds and animals and unarmored men and different kinds of arrows for shooting birds and animals.

When the Tartars go to war they first send scouts who take nothing with them but their tents, horses and weapons. These men seize nothing and do not burn houses or kill animals, but only wound and kill men or, if they cannot do otherwise, put them to flight. The Tartars much prefer to kill them than have them flee. Then the army follows and seizes everything they find, and capture or kill men if they can find them. After this the commanders of the army send skilled raiders everywhere to find men and herds.

Whenever the Tartars come upon rivers they cross them this way even if they are large: most men have a light round leather hide and they make loops all around the edge of it through which they put a cord and tighten it, and thus make a sack which they fill with clothing and other things, and draw it together tightly. After this they put saddles in the middle of them as well as other heavy things. The men sit in the middle of them and tie the boat they have prepared to the tail of a horse. They make one man, swim before the horse and lead it; or they sometimes have two oars and paddle over the water with these and cross the river. In fact, they drive the horses into the water and one man swims next to a horse which he leads and all the other horses follow it, and they cross water and large rivers this way. Other Tartars who are poor have a leather sack sewed up well (everyone must have one) into which they put all their clothing and their possessions and they tie up the mouth of the sack strongly and hang it from the horse's tail and cross as explained above.

You should know that when the Tartars see the enemy they advance and everyone shoots three or four arrows, and if they see that they cannot overwhelm the enemy they go back to their comrades. And this is a trick, so that their adversaries follow them to a place where the Tartars have prepared an ambush. If their enemies follow them to this trap, the Tartars circle around them and wound and kill them. If the Tartars see that the enemy is very numerous, they sometimes turn away for a day or two and invade and despoil a different area and kill men and destroy and lay waste the country. If they find they cannot do this, they sometimes retreat for ten or twelve days and stay in a safe place until their adversaries' army disbands and then they secretly come and depopulate the entire country. The Tartars are the most clever in war, because they have been at war for more than forty years with other people.

When they wish to advance to battle they arrange all their lines just as they are to fight. The generals or princes of the army do not go into the battle, but stay a long way from the enemy and they have boys and women on horses next to them, and sometimes they put dummies of men on horses. They do this so that the number of their soldiers will seem great. The Tartars send a battle line of captives and other people who are among them against the front of the enemy and perhaps some Tartars go with them. They place the other battle groups of the stronger men to the right and left so they will not be seen by their adversaries and thus they circle about the enemy and draw them into the middle and they begin to attack them from all sides. When the Tartars are few in number they use boys and women and horses and dummy men, as stated above, so that they may seem more numerous to their adversaries who are surrounded by them, especially when they see them with the general or prince of the army and think they are soldiers, and are frightened and confused by this. If the enemy fights well the Tartars make way for them to flee; and once they begin to flee and become separated from one another the Tartars attack them and then kill as many in flight as they would in battle.[48] You should know that if they can do otherwise they prefer not to fight hand to hand, but they injure and kill men and horses with arrows, and when the men and horses have been hurt by arrows, then they fall upon them.

The Tartars attack fortifications this way: if a place is well fortified they surround it and securely hedge it in so that no one can get in our out, and they fight fiercely with machines and arrows and do they stop the attack by day nor night, so that those in the fort can not rest. The Tartars do rest however, because they divide up their battalions and one follows the other in fighting so they are not tired at all. If they cannot take the place that way, they throw Greek fire. In fact, they sometimes take the grease of the men they kill and throw it liquefied onto the houses, and wherever this grease catches fire it burns as though it cannot not be extinguished. Yet it may be put out, they say, by pouring wine or beer over it, and if it falls onto flesh it may be extinguished by rubbing it with the palm of the hand.

If the Tartars do not prevail in this way and the city or camp has a river, they block it or they make another riverbed and submerge the fort if they can. If they are unable to do so, however, they tunnel under it and approach it armed from underground. Once they have entered at one place they set fire to it so that it burns while they fight the men of the fort in another area. If, however, they cannot take the place this way, they make their own camp or fort so that they are not troubled by enemy missiles and they shoot against it many times, unless it happens that the army has outside help which

4. Persian painting of Mongols attacking a city.

fights them and removes the Tartars by main force. But when they stand before a fortress, they speak mildly with the people and promise them a great deal so they will surrender. And if they surrender, the Tartars say to them, "Come out so that, according to our custom, we may count you." And when the townspeople come out, the Tartars ask who the craftsmen are among them and put these aside; the others however, except those whom they wish to have as slaves, they kill with their battle axes. It is said that if they spare a few, they never spare the noble or worthy men, and if by chance they do spare some nobles, they may not leave captivity by prayer or ransom.

In their wars they kill whomever they capture, unless by chance they decide to keep them as slaves. They assign those to be killed to captains of hundreds so they may be killed by them with battle axes; these captains then divide the captives as they decide and give ten or more or less to a servant to be killed.

CHAPTER SEVEN

How The Tartars Make Peace, the Countries they have Conquered, the Countries which have Resisted them Successfully, and the Despotism the Tartars Exert over their Subjects

We have described how they fight, so now we must tell about of the countries they have conquered, and we will do it this way: first we shall tell how the Tartars make peace with people, second, the names of the countries which they have conquered, third, the countries which have resisted them strongly, and fourth the despotism which they exercise over them.

You have to know that the Tartars do not make peace with anyone unless they submit to the Tartars because, as we said above, they have Chingis Khan's command and, if they can, they must conquer all other nations.[49] Here is what the Tartars ask from them: that they join the army with them against anyone whenever the Tartars wish, and that they give a tenth of everything the have, both people and property. Therefore the Tartars count ten boys and take one of them, and they do the same with the girls whom they take to their own country and keep as slaves; they count the rest and organize them as is their custom.

But once the Tartars have people in their power, they do not keep any promise they have made to them, they agree in every way they can, but only to take advantage of them. When we were in Russia, a Saracen was sent to us, and it was said he was from Cuyuc Khan and Bati, and this officer took one boy from whomever had three, as was later told to us; and any man who did not have a wife he led away; and he did the same with women who did not have legitimate husbands. He likewise deported paupers and those who begged for their food. However, he counted those remaining according to the Tartar custom, and took note of everyone, the small and the great alike, even babes a day old. Whether rich or poor the people must send this tribute: the pelt of a white bear and of a black beaver and of a black sable and a black pelt of a certain animal which has a den in that country whose name we do not know how to say in Latin (however, the Poles and the Ruthenians call this animal *dochori*) and a black fox pelt. Anyone who does not give this is led to Tartary and becomes a slave.

The Tartars order foreign princes to visit them without delay, and when they arrive they receive none of the honors they are accustomed to, but instead are treated like common people, and they must present the Tartars with many gifts: to the leaders and their wives and to the officers of the thousands and hundreds-- to everyone generally. Even the servants themselves seek gifts with great insistence and not only from them, but even from ambassadors when they are sent to them.

They kill princes sometimes, as we told of Michael and others. However, the Tartars allow some princes to return in order to attract others. They kill some princes with potions or poison. In fact, the Tartars' intention is that they alone should rule the world; to this end they look for opportunities to kill nobles. They keep the sons or brothers of those they allow to return and never send them back again, as was done with the son of Ierozlai and a duke of the Alani and many others. If a father or a brother dies without an heir, they never send the son or brother back, but use any means to take his principality completely away from him, just as we saw done with a certain duke of the Solangi.

The Tartars place their *basckaks*, or prefects, in the territories of those whom they allow to return, and everyone must obey them from the poorest man to the duke. If the men of a certain city or country do not do as he wishes, the *basckak* alleges that they are disloyal, so the Tartars ruin the city or land and kill the men who are in it by their strong hand and they attack suddenly and by surprise by order of the Tartar prince who controls the country. This happened shortly after we had arrived in Tartary to a city in Ruthenia that the Tartars gave to the Kumans. And not only the Tartar prince who took over the land, or his prefect, but any Tartar noble who travels through the town or country does so as though he ruled it, and the more so the greater he is.

What is more the Tartars look for and take without argument gold and silver and other things they want, whenever and however much pleases them. Moreover, if they wish it, the Princes who have submitted must go to the emperor of the Tartars to please him, as recently happened with two sons of the King of Georgia. One son was legitimate and the other, born of adultery, was called David. The legitimate son was named Melic. Their father left part of his land to the bastard son and the other, who was younger, came with his mother to the

Tartars' emperor because David was already on his way there. The mother of this other son (that is, Melic), was of course the Queen of Georgia, and her husband held power through her, because this kingdom was being held through women, but she died on the way. When the sons arrived they gave valuable gifts, especially the legitimate son, who wanted the land that his father had left to David, who should not have had it because he was a bastard. So David replied, "It is true I am the son of a concubine, so I ask that justice be done to me according to the Tartars' custom, who make no distinction between legitimate and illegitimate sons." Thus judgment was given against the legitimate son so that David, who was the elder, prevailed and kept the land quietly and peacefully that his father had given. Thus Melic lost the gifts which he had given and the suit against his brother David.

The Tartars accept tribute from other nations far away from them that are joined to them through other nations, that they fear somewhat and that are not subject to them, and the Tartars pretend to act peacefully so they will not send their armies against the Tartars and so that they will not be afraid to betray themselves to them. This was done with Obesis or Georgia, from which the Tartars accept fifty or forty thousand *yperperum* or bezants as tribute. They allow others to remain in peace yet, as we understand from them, they plan to rebel.

The names of the nations they have conquered are these: the Kytai, Naimani, Solani, Karakytai or Black Kytai, Canana, Tumat, Voyrat, Karaniti, Huyur, Sumoal, Merkits, Mecrits, Sarihuyur, Bascart (that is, Great Hungary), Kergis, Cosmir, the Saracens, Bisermini, Turcomans, Byleri (that is, Great Bulgaria), Corola,

Comuchi, Burithabets, Parossiti, Cassi, Alani (or Assi), Obesi or Georgians, Nestorians, Armenians, Kangiti, Comani, Brutachi (who are Jews), Mandui, Torai, Bazoni, Samogedi, Persians, Tati, India Minor (or Ethiopia), Circassians, Ruthenians, Baghdad, and Sarti. There are many other lands, but we do not know their names. We saw men and women brought from all the lands named above.

Here, however, are the names of the countries which have resisted them stoutly and are not conquered: Greater India, Mangia, a certain part of the Alans, a certain part of the Kytai, and the Saxons. In fact, the Tartars besieged a Saxon town, as was told to us there, and tried to subdue them. The Saxons built machines to use against the Tartars' machines and they destroyed all of the Tartars' machines, nor could they approach the city to fight because of the machines and ballistas; at length they made a tunnel and burst into the city and some tried to burn the city while others fought. However, the townsmen sent one group to extinguish the fire and another group fought stoutly with the Tartars who had entered the city and killed and wounded many compelling them to retreat to their fellows. The Tartars, seeing that they could do nothing to them, and that many men had died, retreated back to them.[50]

In the Saracens' country and others the Tartars act like lords and take all their best craftsmen and make them do all their work. Others, however, give articles of their work to the Tartars as tribute or gather all the grain into their masters' barns. The Tartars, however, give them enough seeds to adequately suffice for their needs. To others however, they give a scant pound of bread a day and nothing else besides a small amount of meat three times a week, though only to those who live in the cities and make these articles. Above all when it pleases a lord, he takes all the young men with their wives and children and makes them travel after him with all his slaves, and they are considered Tartars, but really they are captives, because, even if they are counted among as Tartars they still are not held in the same respect as Tartars, but are regarded as slaves and are sent into every danger as are other captives. These, therefore, are the first in battle, and if a swamp or dangerous water must be crossed, they must be the first to try. They have to do all the work that must be done, and if they offend in any way or do not obey a nod, they are beaten like donkeys.

Briefly, they eat and drink a small amount and they are poorly clothed unless by chance they can work as goldsmiths or other useful tradesmen. But some have such bad masters that they give nothing to them, nor do they have time on account of the many tasks of their masters, to do anything for themselves unless they steal time when they should rest or sleep and this if they are permitted wives and their own camp. Others, however, whom they keep at home as slaves, are filled with every sorrow. For instance, we saw them most often go about in hide trousers with the whole body nude in the greatest heat of the sun, and in winter endure the greatest cold, and we saw them lose feet or the fingers of the hand from the extreme cold. We heard of others dying, or indeed being rendered helpless in all limbs from the cold.

CHAPTER EIGHT

How to Fight the Tartars and what to Expect; the Arms and Organization of such Forces; How to Meet Tartar Cunning in Battle, and how to Supply Fortresses and Cities, and What should be Done with Captives

Now that we have described the lands which obey the Tartars, we must set out how to wage war against them, which, it would seem, is best described in way: first shall tell what the Tartars intend, second the arms and organization of forces, third, how to respond to their cunning in battle, fourth, the fortification of their camps and cities, and fifth, what should be done with captives.

The Tartars mean to conquer the entire world if they can, as we have already said. This is why their emperor heads his letters thus: "The Power of God, the Emperor of all Men" and the superscription of his seal is this: "God in Heaven and Cuyuc Khan over the Earth, the Power of God, the Seal of the Emperor of all Men". And so, as it is said, they do not make peace with anyone unless they submit. Therefore, because except for Christendom, there is no land in the world which they have not taken, they are preparing to fight us. Everyone should know that we lived at the Tartar court where there had been convened a solemn counsel at which it has been decided for many years (we were there when they elected Cuyuc emperor in our presence, who is called Khan in their language) which aforesaid Cuyuc Khan raised his standard, along with those of all his princes, against the Church of God and the Roman Empire, and against all the states of Christendom and the people of the west, unless they do what he has ordered of the Lord Pope and the great men and the whole population of the western Christians[51].

But we should not do this, it seems to us, because of the great and intolerable servitude (such as has not until now been heard of until now) that we saw with our own eyes, to which the Tartars reduce all of their subject peoples, and because the Tartars are a faithless and people cannot trust in their words at all, because whatever they promise they do not observe, when they see chance favor them. The Tartars are dishonest in all their acts and promises; they intend to supplant all the princes, nobles, soldiers and honest men in the world as said above), and they do this by trick and artifice against their subjects, then also because it is not fitting that Christians should submit to the Tartars because of their abominations, and because the worship of God will be reduced to nothing and their souls perish and their bodies be afflicted in an unbelievable number of ways. At first the Tartars are mild, but later they sting and injure like scorpions; and also because they are few in number and weaker in body than the Christian people.

The soldiers and commanders of the army were assigned in this council. Of every ten men they sent along three with his slaves from every land within their power. We were told that one army is to enter through Hungary, and the second through Poland. What is more, they come to fight constantly for eighteen years. That is the time allotted to the campaign. Last March when we passed through Russia we found the army summoned from all the Tartars. Furthermore they will advance in three or four years as far as Comania. From Comania they will attack the lands listed above: we do not know yet whether they will come roughly after the third winter, whether to expect them at that time, or if they will more likely come suddenly.

This is all certain and true unless God, by his grace, puts an obstacle in their path, as he did when they came into Hungary and Poland. They had meant to fight thirty years, but their emperor was poisoned and so they suspended the war until now.[52] Now, however, because a new emperor has been installed, the Tartars have begun to prepare for war. You should know that the emperor said with his own mouth that he wished to send an army into Livonia and Prussia. And because he intends to overthrow the whole world or reduce it to servitude, and because slavery is intolerable to our people, as we said above, we must fight them.

If one province does not wish to cooperate with another, the Tartars will choose to attack that land, and they will use the men whom they capture to fight against another country, and those men will be in the forefront.[53] If they fight badly they will be killed by the Tartars, while if they fight well the Tartars will hold them with promises and praise and indeed, if they do not flee from them, the Tartars will promise to make them great lords. Afterwards, though, when the Tartars are certain that they will not run away, they will make unhappy slaves of them; and as for the women, to those whom they wish to keep as servants and concubines they will do the same thing. Thus, with the men of defeated

5. Chinese painting of a Mongol
and his horse after a hunt.

provinces they will destroy the next country, nor will another province be able to resist them by itself, just as we have seen, unless God wishes to defend them, because, as said above, men are gathered for war from their entire empire. Therefore if the Christians wish to save themselves, their country, and Christianity, they must gather in one body the kings, princes, barons and rectors of the lands and send men to fight the Tartars under a single plan, and before this they should begin to strip the land because after the Tartars are seen in the countryside no one will be able to help to another, because these men will, in companies, seek out and kill men everywhere. And if they close themselves in fortresses, the Tartars place three or four thousand men or more around the fortress or city who besiege it. And they nonetheless will spread through the land killing men.

Whoever wishes to fight the Tartars should have these weapons: a good bow or strong crossbow (which they fear), and enough arrows and a good axe of good iron or a hatchet with a long handle. The points of the arrows for the bow or crossbow should be tempered when they are hot in water mixed with salt, as the Tartars do, so that they should be very strong for penetrating their armor; swords and lances with a hook, which are good for pulling them from the saddle because they fall easily from it, daggers, thick cuirasses because arrows do not easily penetrate these, and a helmet and armor and other things to protect the body and the horse from their weapons and arrows. And if some are not as well armed as we have described, they should stay behind the others, as the Tartars do, and shoot against them with bows and crossbows. Nor should they spare money in buying armor, so they can keep their souls, bodies, freedom and other things.

They should organize their battle groups as the Tartars do, by commanders of thousands, and hundreds, by captains of ten and generals of the army. These generals should not enter the battle, just as Tartar generals do not, but should watch and command the army. They should establish the rule that the men advance to battle at the same time or otherwise, as they are positioned. And whoever abandons his fellow to advance to the battle or to the fighting, or whoever flees unless all retire, should be severely punished; because then part of the Tartar soldiers follow the fugitives and kill them with arrows and part of the Tartars remain with those who fight, and so confuse and kill those staying and fleeing. And likewise whoever loots before the entire enemy army is beaten should be punished the most, for among the Tartars these men are killed without mercy. The battleground should be chosen, if possible, where there is a flat field, so they may see in all directions. And they should have, if possible, a great wood at the back or on the side, because then the Tartars cannot enter between themselves and the wood. Nor should they advance in a single body, but instead they should make up many battle groups divided from each other, but not too far apart. And they should set up a battle line against those who attack first which charges them; and if the Tartars feign flight they must not chase them very far unless they can see well enough lest the Tartars draw them into ambushes as they are accustomed to do. And the other battle groups must be prepared to help that group if there is a chance.

Above all, they must have scouts everywhere who see when other Tartar squadrons come back from the right and left; and they must always send a squadron against the squadron that attacks them. The Tartars always try to surround their enemies, so they must be very careful lest this happen to them because an army is easily defeated this way. The squadrons, however, must be careful of this: not to chase a long way after them because of the traps the Tartars commonly prepare; indeed the Tartars fight more by trickery than strength. The leaders of the army must always be prepared to send help, if necessary, to those in the battle, and therefore they should stay a short distance behind them so their horses do not become tired because we do not have a great number of them. But the Tartar does not mount for three or four days afterwards the horse he has ridden for one day; so they do not ride tired horses because of the great number they have. And if the Tartars retreat, our men should still not pursue and in turn become separated, because the Tartars only pretend to do this so the army will be divided and afterwards they freely attack and destroy the whole country. They must beware and not squander their supplies and so be known to be reduced to poverty and give the Tartars a means to kill them and others and destroy the whole country and because of their squandering allow the name of God to be blasphemed. They must act diligently so that if it happens that some soldiers leave, others take their place.

Our leaders should also mind the army day and night lest the Tartars overcome them quickly and suddenly, because the Tartars, like devils, study many methods of attack. Therefore they must be prepared both night and day nor should they give in to pillage, or sit too long at table and be discovered unprepared, because the Tartars always watch to find a way to attack. Indeed, the men of a country that expects the Tartars or fears that they will come upon them should have secret caches in which to put grain and other things for two reasons: naturally, so the Tartars cannot get it and so, God willing, they can find it later. People fleeing the countryside should burn fodder and straw or hide it well, so that the Tartars' horses find less to eat.

However, if they wish to provision cities and fortresses they should first consider what their positions are: the site of a fortress should be such that they cannot be driven out by catapults and arrows, and it should have enough water and wood, and if it is possible, the entry and exit must be such that they cannot be destroyed and they should have enough men who can fight well. And they must watch carefully lest, by some trick, the Tartars seize th[...] *How they should build Fortresses against Tartars.* e enough supplies for many y[...] care of the supplies carefull[...]ey do not know how long they will be besieged in the fortress because, once they begin, the Tartars besiege a fortress for years, just as there is today in the country of the Alans a fortress on a mountain which, we believe, they have besieged for twelve years; the Alans have resisted strongly and killed many Tartars and nobles.

Fortresses and cities that do not have such sites should be carefully surrounded with deep walled fosses and well built walls, and they should have enough arrows and stones and slingshot. They should be most careful not to allow the Tartars to bring up their catapults, but should drive them away with their own machines. And if it happens through some trick or scheme the Tartars do set up their catapults they should destroy them with their own if they can. They should fight back with crossbows and slings and catapults so the Tartars do not approach the city. They should prepare for other things as stated above. As for fortresses and cities which are situated by rivers, they must carefully see to it that they are not submerged. But it must be known that the Tartars prize it when men lock themselves in towns and fortresses rather then fight them in the field. Indeed they say that these men are little pigs closed in a pen around whom they place guards, as stated above.

If Tartars are thrown from their horses in battle they must be captured at once because when they are on the ground they shoot well and injure and kill horses and men. And if they are caught they should be kept in order to have through them something like a perpetual peace, or else great sums shall be given for them because they value each other so. Therefore when they are captured, if they are taken alive, a strict guard must be kept lest they escape.

The Tartars are to be recognized by their appearance described above. There are many other races with them, who can be distinguished from them by that description. You must also know that there are many in every part of the army with the Tartars who, if they see the chance and believe our men will not kill them, would fight the Tartars as they themselves said to us, and would harm them more than others who are openly their enemies. These things have been written above, as we say, only for the reference of those who see and hear them and not to instruct those people who, by fighting in the army, have learned the skills of war; we believe that no one acts and thinks better than those who are careful and learned; they can yet, through what has been said above, have the chance and the material to understand. As it is written: "He who listens shall be wiser and shall have the knowledge to command."

CHAPTER NINE

The Provinces We Passed Through and their Location; the Court of the Emperor of the Tartars and his Government, and the Witnesses who Met us there

Now that we have told how to wage war against them, we will finally speak of the route we took and of the location of the countries through which we passed, and of the organization of the emperor's court and his government and of the witnesses who met us in the Tartars' country.

After we had decided, as explained earlier, to travel to the Tartars, we went to the King of the Bohemians. We took his advice about which route was best for us to travel because we had known this lord for a long time. He told us it seemed best to him to travel through Poland and Russia. Indeed, he had relatives in Poland whose help we could have in entering Russia, and when he had given us his letters and a safe conduct we took up the route through Poland. He paid our expenses through his lands and cities until we came to Duke Boleslav of Silesia, his nephew, who was familiar and well known to us. He also gave us letters and a safe conduct and expenses through his holdings and cities until we came to Duke Conrad of Lanciscia. At this point God favored us and Lord Vasilco, Duke of Russia, arrived there and we learned a great deal about the Tartars from him. What is more, he sent his envoys back, and they returned to him and his brother Daniel[54] and brought a safe conduct to travel to Bati, Daniel's lord. Duke Vasilco told us that if we wished to visit we must have great gifts to give them because they demanded them avidly, and if they were not given (and it is true) an ambassador could not carry out his mission to them effectively; in fact he would be deemed worthless.

Because we did not want the embassy of the Lord Pope and of the Church to be impeded by this, we bought some pelts of beaver and other animals from the money given to us as charity to live on. Duke Conrad and the Duchess of Cracow and certain knights and the Bishop of Cracow, when they learned this, gave us even more of these pelts. Duke Conrad, his son, the Duke of Cracow and the Bishop and barons of Cracow implored Duke Vasilco to help us as much as he could to get to the Tartars. Duke Vasilco replied that he would do it gladly, so he took us with him into his country and while he detained us some days at his expense so that we might rest a little, he made his bishop come to us as we asked. We read him the letters of the Lord Pope in which he warned them that they[55] should return to the unity of the Holy Mother Church. In fact, we warned them and induced, as far as we could, both the duke as well as the bishops and others who came to do this. When Duke Vasilco had gone to Poland his brother Duke Daniel had gone to Bati and was not present, so they could not answer absolutely, but their reply should be expected at the plenary.

After this Duke Vasilco sent a servant with us as far as Kiev; nevertheless we always travelled in deadly danger because of the Lithuanians who often carry out secret attacks as far as they are able over Russian territory, especially in the area through which we had to pass, and because most of the Russian men have been killed or captured by the Tartars they can hardly resist them. We were safe from the Ruthenians, however, because of this servant. Therefore, thanks to the grace of God, we were spared from the enemies of the Cross of Christ and came to Kiev which is Russia's great city.

When we arrived there, we consulted about our route with a millenarius and other nobles who were there. They told us that if we led the horses we had into Tartary, they would not know how to dig grass from beneath the snow when it was deep, as Tartar horses do, and it would not be possible to find anything else for them to eat because the Tartars have neither straw nor hay nor fodder, and they would all die. So, we talked among ourselves and told the two boys who looked after them to send them away. Then we had to give the millenarius gifts to win his favor so he would give us proper horses and a safe conduct. Furthermore, before we had arrived in Kiev we were deathly sick in Danilova.

Even so we had ourselves drawn in a cart through the snow in extreme cold lest the embassy of the Lord Pope and Christianity be impeded. After all this business had been done in Kiev, on the second day after the Feast of the Purification of our Lord, we took up the road to the barbarian nations with the horses of the millenarius and the safe conduct from Kiev.

We came to a certain village which was directly under the control of a Tartar called Canova. The prefect of this town gave us horses and a pass to another village in which there was an Alan prefect called Micheas who was wicked and worthless. This fellow had sent some of his men to us in Kiev who told us falsely, as though on behalf of Corenza, that if we were ambassadors, we must come to him. He did this, even though it was untrue, so that he could extort gifts from us. Thus when we arrived, he gave us a great deal of trouble and unless we promised him gifts, he would not help us at all. So, seeing that otherwise we could not proceed further, we promised to give him some gifts, but when we gave what seemed right he would not accept them until we gave more. Thus we had to add as much as he liked, and he stole from us dishonestly, secretly and wickedly.

After this we left with him on the second feast day of Quinquegesima and he led us to the first Tartar sentinel. And when we camped on Prima Sexta after Ash Wednesday at sunset, armed Tartars rushed upon us, and asked who we were. After we replied that we were emissaries of the Lord Pope and they had accepted some food from us, they went straight away.

The next day came and we rose and had travelled a bit when the officials who were in charge of the area came to us and asked why we came to them and what our business was. We told them that we were emissaries of the Lord Pope who was the lord and father of the Christians and who had sent us, both to the king and the princes and to all Tartars because he wished all Christians to be the Tartars' friends and be at peace with them. Moreover he wished the Tartars to be glorified in the eyes of God in heaven. Therefore, the Lord Pope warned them both through us and by his letters that they should become Christians and accept the faith of God and Our Lord Jesus Christ because otherwise they could not be saved. The Pope remarked also that he was appalled at such a slaughter of men, mostly of Christians and principally of Hungarians, Moravians and Poles, who were subject to them, that the Tartars had done when these people had not hurt or tried to hurt them. And because God was seriously angered by this, the Pope warned them that they should avoid similar deeds and do penance for their actions. We added to this that the Lord Pope asked them to write down to him what else they planned to do and what their intentions were, and how they replied to everything said to them in these letters.

When they had heard our position and understood it, the Tartars said they wished to deliberate and they offered us their horses and a guide to Corenza and right away sought gifts, which we gave them; we needed to show our good will. When the gifts had been given and we had accepted their horses (from which they themselves climbed down), we took up the road to Corenza with their guide. The Tartars rode quickly using whips, as we have described, and sent a messenger to this commander. This commander moreover was the lord of everybody who was stationed against the men of the west, to prevent them from attacking suddenly and impulsively. We heard that this officer commanded six thousand armed men.

When we arrived, Corenza made us pitch our camp a long way from him and sent us his servants who asked us what we wished to bow with, which means: "What gifts do you wish to give him?" We replied that the Lord Pope did not send any gifts because he was not certain that we could journey to him. What is more, we had passed through very dangerous places and feared the Lithuanians who often travelled the roads from Poland almost to the Tartar territory, along which we had to make our way. "Nevertheless, from what we have to feed ourselves by the grace of God and our Lord the Pope, so far as we are able, we will honor him." And when we had given him many things, it was still not enough and he sought more through agents, and promised he would treat us well if we met his demands which we could not refuse if we wished to survive and carry out properly the embassy of the Lord Pope.

After he had taken the gifts, the Tartars led us to their horde, or camp, and we were instructed to bow three times with the left knee before the door of the tent and to be quite certain not to step on the threshold of the doorway, which we were careful not to do, because the penalty is death for those who knowingly tread on the threshold of any leader. After this we entered, as ordered, and knelt as we said above to the leader in person and all his important men who were specially called there for the occasion. We also gave him the Lord Pope's letters, but because our interpreter, whom we had already paid and led from Kiev was not skilled enough to translate the letters (and there was no one else fit to be had), they could not be translated. When this was over, horses were given to us along with three Tartars, two of whom were decani and the other one of Bati's men, who took us quickly to this prince. Bati is the most powerful of all the Tartar princes except for the emperor whom even he must obey.

On the second feast day which is after the first Sunday of Quadragesima, we took the road to Bati and rode as fast as the horses could go at a trot, because we had fresh horses three or four times almost every day. We rode from morning until it was almost night, yet we could not get there for the greater part of four weeks.

We travelled through all the country of the Comani, which is completely flat, and which has four great rivers.

The first is called the Neper, along which is the part of Russia that Corenza rules and another area of flatlands where Mouci rules who is more powerful than Corenza. The second is the Don over which rules a certain prince who is married to Bati's sister, called Carbon. The third is the Volga and this river, along which Bati rules, is very large. The fourth is called the Iaec, over which two millenarii rule, one over one part and the other over another. All of these flow to the sea in winter and in summer they overflow their banks up to the hills. In fact this sea is the Great Sea from which extends the Arm of St. George which goes to Constantinople. Along the Neper, however, we spent many days on ice. These rivers are big and full of fish and greater than the Volga. These rivers enter the Greek Sea which is called the Great Sea, and we travelled along the shores of that sea which is quite dangerous because of ice in many places. It was well frozen from the shore to a distance of three leagues inland.

However, before we had come to Bati, two of our Tartars went ahead and related to him all that we had said to Corenza, and when we came to Bati, in the land of the Comani, we were stationed a good league from his camp. When we were taken to his court we were told that we must walk between two fires, which we did not wish to do at all. But the Tartars said to us, "You will be safe; we only make you pass between two fires so that if you plan any evil for our lord, or if you bring any poison, the fire will carry it away." We replied, "Because we do not wish to be mistrusted for it we will do so."

When we had come to the horde we were asked by an officer of Bati named Eldegai what we wished to bow with, that is, what presents we wished to offer. We replied as we had earlier to Corenza and said, of course, that the Lord Pope had not sent any gifts, but that from what we had by the grace of God and our Lord Pope for expenses, we wished to honor him as far as we were able. After the gifts had been given and accepted, his officer (who was called Eldegai) asked us why we had come. We gave him the same reasons we had given to Corenza.

After he had heard our explanation Eldegai brought us into camp after we had first bowed and listened to the warning about the threshold, as we have said. So, as we entered, we knelt and said our piece. When we had spoken, we gave over the letters and asked that an interpreter be given to us who could translate them, and two were given to us, and we carefully translated the letters with them into Ruthenian, into Saracen, and then into the Tartar language. The translation was given to Bati who read and considered it carefully. At length we were taken back to our camp, but the Tartars gave us no food except a very small amount of millet in a shallow bowl when we arrived that first night.

This Bati is quite magnificent, he levies taxes and has officials just as if he were emperor. Indeed he sits in the highest place, as on a throne, with one of his wives. All others, however, whether brothers or sons and other nobles sit below in the middle on a bench. The other men sit beyond them on the ground, with the men on the right and the women on the left. He has great and beautiful tents of linen which belonged to the King of Hungary[56]. No one outside of the tents dares approach, except the family, unless he is summoned, no matter how great and powerful he may be, unless he knows it is Bati's wish. However, after we had given our explanation, we sat on the left as do all ambassadors when they come, but in returning from the emperor we were always placed on the right. In the middle, before the door of the tent, a table was set on which was placed drink in gold and silver vessels. Not once did Bati drink, or any of the princes of the Tartars, especially in public, except when they were sung to or acclaimed. When he rides, a canopy or little tent is carried over his head on a spear point, and most of the great princes of the Tartars do this and so do their wives. This Bati is very good to his people, yet they fear him greatly. He is most savage in battle and very wise and most clever in war because he has fought so much.

On the day of the Holy Sabbath we were called to the camp and the aforesaid official of Bati came out and said on his behalf that we must go to the Emperor Cuyuc. Certain of our people were kept back in their country on the pretext that the Tartars wished to send them to the Lord Pope. We gave them letters stating everything that had happened but when they had gone only as far as Mouci, he kept them in his territory until our return.

So, on the day of the Resurrection of Our Lord, after the order was given and we had had some food, we went off with the two Tartars who were assigned to us by Corenza. We left with many tears not knowing whether we travelled towards death or life. Moreover, we were so ill we could hardly ride; during the whole of Lent our only food had been millet with water and salt and on other fasting days the same, and we did not have anything to drink besides snow melted in a cooking pot.

Directly north of Comania, immediately past Russia are the Mordvins, Belorus, that is Greater Bulgaria, the Bascarti, that is Greater Hungary. After the Bascarti, the Parossiti and Samogedi, after the Samogedi are people at the edge of the ocean bordering a wasteland who are said to have dog's faces. To the south there are the Alans, Circassians, Gazarenes, Greece, Constantinople, and the land of the Hileri, the Tartars, the Brutachi who are said to be Jews (they shave the head) and the land of the Sicciri and the Georgians and Armenians and the land of the Turks. To the West are Hungary and Russia. This land is great and wide.

We travelled quickly because we had fresh horses every day: five in a day or seven, though not when we went through a wasteland, as we said above, and then we took better, stronger horses which could bear continuous work, and we rode from the beginning of Quinquegesima until eight days after Easter. The Tartars have killed these Comani; some have fled from them and others are reduced to their service. However, many who fled have returned to them.

After this we entered the country of the Kangiti, which is very lacking in water in many places where men die from the lack of water. That is why many of the Russian Duke Ierozlai's men, who went to him in the Tartars' country, died in this desert from thirst. In this country and in Comania we found many skulls and bones of men lying about in heaps over the ground. We went through this land from the eighth day after Easter until almost Ascension Day. These men are pagans and neither the Comani nor Kangiti work, but live only from animals, nor do they build houses, but live in tents. The Tartars have supplanted these people and live in their land, and those who remain are reduced to their service.

From the land of the Kangiti we entered the land of the Bisermini. These people used to speak Coman and still do, but they are Muslims. In this country we came upon innumerable destroyed cities, destroyed forts and

6. A Mongol *paiza*, or tablet of authority,
found in the former lands of the Golden Horde
Batu Khan's appanage.

many deserted villages. In this country there is a certain large river whose name we do not know, upon which stands a city called Ianikint, and another called Barchin and another called Ornas and many others whose names we do not know. This land had a ruler who was known as Altisoldan, whose real name we do not know, and who was killed by the Tartars along with all his off-spring. This country has great mountains. To the south lies Jerusalem, Baghdad and the whole land of the Saracens; in this area live the Princes Burin and Cadan who are half brothers. To the north is the land of the Black Kytai and the ocean. Siban lives there who is Bati's brother. We travelled through it from the Feast of the Ascension almost to the eighth day before the Feast of John the Baptist.

After this we entered the land of the Black Kytai in which they have built a completely new city which is called Emil where the emperor has built his house and where we were called in to drink. The emperor's representative made the important people of the city and his two sons publicly applaud us.

We left there and came upon a certain sea, not very large, whose name, because we did not ask, we do not know. On the shore of this sea, however, is a small mountain in which they say there is a cave from which such a strong blast of wind blows in winter that men can hardly pass it and then only with great danger. In summer the sound of the wind is always heard there, though it blows from the cave softly. We travelled along the shore of this sea for many days. This sea has many islands and we passed it on our left. This country, moreover, abounds in rivers, though not large ones. On the shores of the rivers there are forests on every side, though they are not wide. In this land lives Ordu who, because he is the elder brother of Bati, is the eldest of all the Tartar princes, and this is the horde or court of his father where one of his wives rules. The custom among the Tartars is that the court of the princes and the nobles is not broken up, but women are always chosen to rule them and they are given part of the wealth just as their lord was accustomed to do.

After this we came to the first horde of the emperor where one of his wives lives, but because we had not yet seen the emperor they did not wish to call on us or introduce us to their horde, but they had us well served in our tent according the Tartar custom and kept us there a day so that we could rest.

We continued onward on the Vigil of Saint Peter and entered the land of the Naimans, who are pagans. On the Day of the Apostles Peter and Paul a heavy snow fell and we were very cold. This land is hilly and cold and few plants grow there (and these two peoples do not work, but, like the Tartars, live in tents which the carry about) and we travelled through it for many days.

Then we entered the land of the Mongols whom we call the Tartars. We believe that we travelled through this land for three weeks riding hard, and on the day of Saint Mary Magdalene we came to Cuyuc who is now the emperor. We rushed along the entire road because this was our Tartars' order and they quickly led as to the High Council which had gathered now for several years for the election of the emperor, so that we could arrive timely. Therefore, we rose in the morning and travelled until night without eating and often arrived so late that we did not eat in the evening, but what we were supposed to eat in the evening was given to us in the morning. We travelled as much as the horses could trot. The horses were not spared at all because we always had fresh ones and those that tired we left behind, as explained above, so that we rode fast and without any break.

When we arrived, Cuyuc had a tent and expenses given to us, such as the Tartars are accustomed to do; however they did better by us than by other ambassadors. We were not summoned to him because he had not yet been elected, nor had he taken up the imperial office. However, the translation of the letter from the Lord Pope and the speech which we made to Bati were sent to him. After we had waited there five or six days, Cuyuc sent us to his mother where a court was solemnly held, and when we had arrived there, so great was the size of the tent which was made of white fabric, that we reckon that it could hold more than two thousand men. Around it was a hoarding of wood which was painted with various pictures. On the second or third day we went there with the Tartars who were assigned to look after us, and all of the leaders gathered there and each one rode in with his men through the surrounding hills and plain.

On the first day everyone dressed in purple coats and on the second in red and then when Cuyuc came to the tent on the third day everyone dressed in blue and on the fourth day in their best silk. In the hoarding before the tent were two large gates; through one only the emperor could enter, and there was no guard at it even though it was open because no one dared go in or out of it. All who were admitted would enter at the other gate, and at this one there were guards with swords and bows and arrows, and when anyone approached the tent beyond the border where they were placed, if they were caught they were beaten and if they fled they were shot, though the arrows were untipped. Horses were kept two bow shots away. Leaders from everywhere went about with armed men, but only about ten could go as far as the horses and those who tried to do otherwise were severely beaten. And there were many who had on their reins, breastplates, saddles and cruppers, we reckon, about twenty marks of gold. And so the leaders spoke below the tent and, we believe, wrangled over the election. Everyone else was outside of this hoarding, and they waited there until almost noon and then began to drink mares' milk and they drank it until evening which was amazing to see. They called us inside and give us ale because we did not like mares' milk in the least; and so did us a great honor. But still they compelled us to drink so much that we could not stay at all sober, so we complained that this bothered us, but still they continued to force us.

Outside there were Duke Ierozlai of Russian Suzdal and many Kytai and Solangi dukes and two of the sons of the King of Georgia, the ambassador of the Caliph of Baghdad who was a sultan, and more than ten other Saracen sultans, which we believe and which was told us by officials. Indeed there were more than four thousand ambassadors among them who brought tribute and gifts, and sultans and other dukes who came to submit as well as those whom the Tartars had sent for and those who are governors of territories. The Tartars stationed all of them together beyond the hoarding and ordered them to drink together; they always gave a better place to Duke Ierozlai and us when we were outside with them. We think, if we remember rightly, that we were there a good four weeks, and we believe that the election was celebrated there, if not announced there; and therefore it was widely believed to have happened every time that Cuyuc left the tent and so he was hailed by pretty virgins in scarlet wool clothes. They bowed to him, which was not done to any other leader however long he waited outside. They called this the Sira Horde.

We left there and everyone rode together to another place about three or four leagues away where there was another tent prepared in a beautiful plain next to a river between hills, which they call the golden horde, where Cuyuc was to be enthroned on the day of the Assumption of Our Lord. But because hail had fallen (it was mentioned above), this was delayed. The tent was supported by columns which were covered with gold leaf affixed with golden nails and other woods and the ceiling above and the interior of the walls were made of a silken fabric though the exterior was of woolen cloth. We stayed there until the Feast of Saint Bartholomew while a great multitude gathered. And they stood facing south and there were certain people a stone's throw away from the others who walked constantly making long speeches, and kneeling to the south. We, however, who did not know whether they made incantations and knelt to God or to other things did not want to genuflect. When they had done this a long while they returned to the tent and placed Cuyuc on the imperial throne and the leaders knelt to him in public and after this all of the people knelt, except we who were not his subjects. They then began to drink and, as their custom is, they drank continuously until evening. After this they ate cooked meat without salt brought out on carts and the Tartars would give a haunch to each four or five people. Inside, however, they gave meat and broth with salt or seasoning, as they do when they celebrate.

We were called there before the emperor himself and when the secretary Cingai had written our names and those by whom we were sent, and those of the leaders of the Solani and others, he called these out in a loud voice before the emperor and all of the leaders. This done, each one of us bent the left knee four times and they warned us not to touch the inside threshold. And when the Tartars had searched us carefully for knives and found none, we entered the doorway on the eastern side because no one except the emperor alone dares enter by the western side, even a leader to whom a tent belongs. The common people however do not observe this custom much. And this was the first time we entered his camp after he had been made emperor. Cuyuc received all the ambassadors there, but only a few entered the tent.

There were so many gifts given, in silk, in samite, rich cloth and silken cloth and silken belts worked with gold, rich furs and other gifts that it was wonderful to see. A canopy or little tent to be carried over the head of the emperor was presented to him there which was covered all over with gems. And there was a particular provincial governor who gave many camels to him, caparisoned with silken fabric and saddles with certain structures in which men could sit (and we believe there were forty or fifty of them) and many armored horses and mules, some with leather, some with iron. Of course we were asked whether we wished to give gifts but we had used up almost all we had so that we had little to give. More than fifty wagons were placed beyond a hill a long way from the camp and they were all filled with gold and silver and silk clothing which were divided between the emperor and his nobles. And the nobles individually divided their share between their men as it pleased them.

Leaving there, we came to another place where a wonderful tent was set, all of precious red fabric, which

the Kytai had given him, and there we were taken inside.
Each time we entered they gave us ale or wine to drink;
cooked meat was offered to us if we wished to have it.
A canopy of wood was prepared above the emperor's
throne. The throne was entirely of ebony and wonder-
fully carved. There were gold and precious stones and,
if we remember rightly, pearls, and it was mounted by
steps and was rounded at the back. There were benches
placed around the seat and the ladies would sit on stools
on the left side, while on the right side no one sat as
high, and the leaders sat on lower benches, in the
middle and the others sat behind them. And every day
a great number of lords arrived.

These three tents, which we have described above,
were very large. Cuyuc's wives had other tents, however,
of white felt which were quite large and beautiful. Then
the emperor and his mother separated: the emperor's
mother went to one area and the emperor to another to
judge cases. The emperor's aunt who had killed his
father with poison at the time when his army was in
Hungary, so that the army, which was in the lands
described above, withdrew, was caught. For this, she
and many others were judged and killed.

It was at this time that Ierozlai died, the Grand
Duke of that part of Russia called Suzdal. He was
summoned to the emperor's mother who gave him food
and drink from her own hand as though it were an
honor. Then he returned to his lodgings, incontinent
and sick, and was dead in seven days, and all of his body
had in some remarkable way turned grey. Thus everyone believed that he had been poisoned there, so that
the Tartars could seize his land easily. And further it
was said of the sick man, that while his men did not
know of it, the emperor sent a fast messenger into

Russia to his son Alexander[57] asking that he come to him because he wished to give him his father's land. Alexander said he wished to go, but remained. And then the emperor sent letters that if he should come he would have his father's land. Everyone believed though, that the Tartars would kill him if he came or hold him captive forever.

When Ierozlai had died, our Tartars led us to the emperor, if we remember this time correctly, and when the emperor had heard through our Tartars that we had come, he ordered us to return to his mother, because he wished next day to raise his standard against all of the west, which was plainly said to us by those who knew, as was said above. He did not want us to know this, however. And when we were sent back we remained for a few days and were again led back to him where we remained pretty much throughout the month in such hunger and thirst that we could hardly live, because the provisions which were given for four were hardly sufficient for one, and we could not find anything to buy because the market was so far away. Unless God had not sent us a certain Ruthenian called Cosmas (who had been chosen as the emperor's goldsmith) who supported us somewhat, or if God had not helped is in some other way, we would have died.

This man showed us the emperor's throne which he himself had made before Cuyuc was enthroned, and his seal which he had made and explained to us the superscription of his seal, and many other secrets which we had to know. We discovered at the court of this emperor people who had come with other leaders: many Ruthenians, Hungarians, people who knew Latin and French, and Ruthenian clerics and others who had been with the Tartars, some for thirty years, in wars and other circumstances who knew everything about them because they knew the language and had stayed with them constantly, some twenty years, some ten, some more, some less, from whom we could investigate everything. And these men explained everything to us willingly at any time without being asked because they knew what we wanted.

After this the emperor sent us his secretary Cingai, and asked that we write down our words and business and give it to him; we did so and we wrote for him everything we had said to Bati earlier, just as we said above. After several days had passed the emperor had us called again and told us through Kadac, the minister of the entire empire, and before Bala and the secretary Cingai and many other scriveners, to write everything that we had said, which we did gladly and freely. An interpreter was given to us who was good at this as at other things: Temer, a soldier of Ierozlai, one of his clerics and another cleric in the emperor's service. The emperor then asked if the Lord Pope had people who understood Ruthenian or Saracen or even Tartar. We replied to him that we did not understand Ruthenian or Tartar or Saracen, and though there were Saracens in our part of the world, they were distant from the Lord Pope. We said, however, that it seemed to us expedient that they should write in Tartar and explain it to us and we would write it carefully in our script and bear the letter and translation to the Lord Pope. And then they left us to return to the emperor.

However, on Saint Martin's day we were called and Kadac, Cingai, and Bala and the scriveners came to us and gave us the letter of the text which was to be translated from one language to the other. And when we had written it in Latin they read it for themselves by interpreting single words, wanting to know if we strayed in any word. And when both letters were written they made us read them once and twice lest we had not understood something, and they said to us: "See that you understand everything well because it is useless if you do not understand something since you must travel to such distant lands." And when we replied "We understand everything well," the letters were re-written in Saracen in case someone could be found in those parts to read them if the Lord Pope wishes.

The custom of the Tartar emperor is that no stranger may speak to him, no matter how great, except through an intermediary, and it is said he hears and replies through an intermediary. Whenever people proposed business before Kadac, or heard the emperor's reply, his subjects knelt right up to the end of the speech, no matter how great they were. Nor can anyone, because it is not the custom, discuss a matter further, after the emperor has decided it. This emperor, moreover, had a minister, a secretary and scriveners, and thus had all the officials for both public and private business, except lawyers because everything is done in accordance with the emperor's will without the racket of judges. Other princes of the Tartars, as far as these things go, do the same.

This emperor, must be forty or forty-five years old, or more, is of medium height, very wise and extremely clever and very serious, and strict in his morals, so that no one ever easily sees him laugh or make a joke, as Christians told us who had stayed with him constantly. Also, Christians who were of the emperor's household told us they firmly believed that he would become a Christian and that they had an obvious sign of this because he himself supported Christian clerics and paid

7. An Imperial Mongol Seal.

their expenses, and he always had a Christian choir
before his largest tent, and they sang publicly and
openly, and rang the hours according the Greek custom,
as other Christians do, whenever there is a large gather-
ing of Tartars or other foreigners, which the other dukes
do not do.

The emperor proposed to send his own ambassadors
with us because, as the Tartars said to us, they ought to
accompany us. We think they wanted us to ask it of the
Emperor, because one of our Tartars (the one who was
older) told us to ask it. But we saw no advantage to us
by their coming, so we replied that it was not our wish,
but that if the emperor himself of his own desire should
send them, we hoped to conduct them there safely, God
helping. However, for several reasons it seemed to us
they should not come: First, because we feared that if
they saw the dissensions and wars among us they would
think more of attacking us. Second, because we feared
that they would scout our lands. Third, we feared they
would be killed, because our people are for the most
part arrogant and proud. When the servants who were
with us came to the Cardinal who was the Legate of
Germany, and dressed at his request in Tartar clothing,
they were nearly stoned in the road by the Germans and
were driven to strip off their clothing. It is the custom
of the Tartars never to make peace with those men who
kill their ambassadors, and they seek revenge for such
things. Fourth, we feared that they would kidnap us, as
was done to a certain prince of the Saracens, who was
held captive until his death, as is sometimes done. Fifth,
their arrival would be of no use when they had no task
or power other than to bring letters of the emperor to
the Lord Pope and to other princes which we did not

have and we thought about the trouble which could arise from this. Therefore we did not want them to come.

On the third day after this, actually on Saint Britis's day, the Tartars gave us a pass and a letter signed with the imperial seal, that came to us from the emperor's mother. She gave each one of us a fox skin cloak which had the fur outside and which was sewn inside with silken fabric and a fine piece of cloth, some of each of which our Tartars stole (and of that given to the servants they stole the better part), which displeased us, but we did not wish to complain about it.

Then we took up the way back and travelled through the entire winter, often sleeping in wastelands in the snow, where we could make a place in the snow with our feet because there were no trees but only a flat plain; and we often found ourselves completely covered with snow when the wind blew. And when we came to Bati on the day of the Ascension of Our Lord, we told him what the emperor had replied to the Lord Pope, and he said that he did not wish to inquire about anything except what the emperor had written. He said, however, that we should carefully tell the Lord Pope and other powerful men all that the emperor had written. And after he had given us safe conducts, we withdrew from him and went as far as Mouci on the Sabbath in Pentecost Week where our comrades and servants, who had been held there, were returned to us.

From there we went to Corenza who once again sought gifts from us, but we did not give him anything because we did not have anything. He gave us two Comans who were numbered among the Tartars, as far as Russian Kiev. Our Tartar did not dismiss us, however, until we left the last Tartar outpost. These others who were given to us by Corenza did not lead us for six days from the last outpost to Kiev. However we arrived there fifteen days after the Feast of John the Baptist. The Kievans, moreover, when they noticed our arrival, all ran out to us happily. They congratulated us as though we had returned from death. So they did to us through all Poland, Bohemia and Russia.

Daniel and his brother Vasilco gave us a great feast and held us, against our will, for a good eight days. Meanwhile we held a meeting with them and their bishop and other upright men about those things we had discussed before we had travelled to the Tartars, and they all replied that they wished to obey the Lord Pope and have him as a special lord and father and to accept the Holy Roman Church in power and majesty, confirming everything about these things which had been communicated to them earlier by this abbot. To this end he sent ambassadors and his letters with us to the Lord Pope.[58]

So there is no doubt that we have been to the Tartars, as some call them, we have written down the names of those whom we met there: the Russian king Daniel (and all his soldiers and men who travelled with him) found us near the camps of Carbon who is married to Bati's sister. At Corenza's we met Hongrot, a Kievan centurion, and his men who led us some of the way; and they went after us as far as Bati. At Bati's we met a son of the Duke Ierozlai who had with him a Russian soldier who was called Sangor who was of the Coman nation but now is a Christian and another Ruthenian who was our translator at Bati's, from Suzdal. At the court of the Emperor of the Tartars we met Duke Ierozlai who died there and his soldier who is called Temer who was our translator to Cuyuc Khan, the Tartar Emperor, both in translating the letters of the emperor to the Lord Pope and in words said and replied. There was Dubazlaus the cleric of the aforesaid duke, Jacob, Michael and another Jacob, his servant. While returning across the land of the Bisermini, at the city of Ianikint, we met Coligneus who, by order of the wife of Ierozlai and Bati went to the aforesaid Ierozlai and Cocceleban and all his company. All of these have returned to the country of Suzdal in Russia, from whom one can, if necessary, check the truth. At Mouci's we met our companions who had remained, Duke Ierozlai and his company, a certain duke in Russia, Santopolcus by name, and his company. And leaving Comania we met Duke Roman who was going to the Tartars with his retinue, and Duke Oleg who was leaving with his. In fact the ambassador of the Duke of Chernegov left Comania with us and went a long way through Russia with us, and all of these are Ruthenian dukes.

All the city of Kiev which gave us a safe conduct and horses up to the first Tartar guard is a witness, and at our return they took us with a Tartar conduct and their horses which were returned to them. And there are all the Russians past whom we made the trip, who received the signed letters and order of Bati that they should give us money and horses, for if they did not he would have killed them.

Above all there are the merchants of Bratislava who accompanied us to Kiev and know we entered the hand of the Tartars; and many other merchants in Poland as well as Austria, who went to Kiev after we went to the Tartars. There are witnesses and merchants from Constantinople who went past the Tartars into Russia and who were in Kiev when we returned from the Tartar country. The names of these merchants are: Michael the Genoese, and Bartholomew, Manuel the Venetian,

Jacob Renerius of Acre, Nicholas the Pisan, these were the more important; other lesser ones were Marchus, Henry, John, Vasius, another Henry called Bonadea, and Peter of Paschainus. There were many others, but we do not know their names.

We ask all those who have read the above, to neither demean nor disregard it because, as God is our witness, we have written, with truth leading the way, everything that we saw, or heard from others that we judged worthy of belief, and have not knowingly added anything. But because those past whom we made our way in Poland, Bohemia, Germany and in Leodio and Campania, have freely had the story, they wrote it down before it was complete and so it is much shorter, because we did not then have a chance to fully complete it. Therefore no one should marvel because there are many and better corrections in it, seeing that now we have some leisure, we have corrected it fully and perfectly so that it is better than when it was not yet finished.

This ends the story of the Mongols whom we call the Tartars.

NOTES

1. John of Plano Carpini, ca. 1180-1252; Plano Carpini is a small town in Tuscany now called Piano della Maggiore.

2. A reference to the Mongol invasion of Poland and Hungary in 1241.

3. Chinese.

4. All Muslim peoples generally, whether Persians, Turks or Arabs.

5. Uighurs, a somewhat settled Turkic steppe people from whom the Mongols later adopted writing.

6. A steppe people of Central Asia.

7. The Mongol capital city in Central Asia, generally called Karakorum, now abandoned. Originally the capital of the Uighur Turks, it was enlarged, walled and established as the Mongol capital by Occodai, son of Chingis Khan in 1235.

8. Or Yellow Horde, the Great Khan's personal camp outside of Karacorum.

9. The Mongols were well known for shaving the head except for a topknot or scalp-lock, a style later adopted by the Cossacks who settled in some of their territories.

10. These round homes were called "gers", or sometimes by mistake "yurts" which actually refers to the entire camp.

11. Carpini's statement that the "Tartars believe in one God" is inconsistent; he goes on to say that the sun and moon are also held to be deities. In fact the Mongols believed that the supreme deity was the Blue Sky, or Tengri, but they were animists prepared to propitiate the innumerable spirits which they took to inhabit the

world around them. Their priests were shamans, but the office is here translated as "sorcerer" since Carpini himself apparently saw them in this way. He uses the term *incantator* to describe them.

12. Prince Michael of Chernigov's death was probably politically rather than religiously motivated since he had earlier been involved with Daniel of Galicia and Andrei of Vladimir-Suzdalia in resisting the Mongols. Michael's refusal to submit to Mongol shamanist ritual may have been a political statement masked as a religious objection, see C. J. Halperin, *The Tatar Yoke*, Slavica Publishers, Inc, Columbus, OH, 1985, pp 49-51. The manner of killing him was chosen because the Mongols had a superstitious aversion to shedding royal blood except in battle.

13. Comani: Kumans or Kipchaks, a Turkic people of the Russian steppe amalgamated into the Mongol nation during the campaign against the Russian principalities, 1236-1238.

14. The location of the tomb of Jinghiz Khan, for example, is unknown.

15. Yaroslav, Grand Duke of Chernikov, 1238-1247, father of Alexander Nevsky, the Russian national hero.

16. There is no indication, whatever bad points the Tartars possessed, that cannibalism was among them.

17. Yekka Mongols: the tribe into which Chingis Khan was born.

18. Tartars: or Tatars, these people were said to have been almost entirely killed off by Chingis Khan in revenge for murdering his father.

19.   Mecrits: probably a corruption of Merkits, a tribe early consolidated by Chingis Khan into the Mongols.

20.   Chingis: born Temujin around 1162 he took the title Jinghiz Khan, probably in 1189, after consolidating his hold over the steppe tribes of Central Asia.

21.   Karakytai: a sinicized steppe people living on the western borders of China.

22.   For a similar amusing story see Caesar's *Gallic Wars* where he describes Germans hunting elks which have no knees and cannot rise when they fall.

23.   Christians of the Nestorian sect were fairly common among the steppe peoples. The Nestorians had fled persecution in the Byzantine Empire by heading into Asia. Cut off from the Christian world for centuries their religion would have differed a great deal from the Christianity familiar to Carpini.

24.   Stories of voluntary cannibalism cannot be credited. Carpini may well have been told such stories by Mongols seeking to enhance their reputation for ferocity, but the Mongol army in Chingis Khan's day was largely voluntary with soldiers equipping themselves and even paying for the privilege of service in the expectation of plunder.   Under these conditions this story, incredible anyway, becomes even more unlikely.   It is also inconsistent with Carpini's statement in Chapter Eight that the Mongols valued each other so that they would pay great ransoms for prisoners of war.

25.   Carpini refers to him as "Iohannes Presbyter", literally "Bishop John" though he is more generally known as the mythical king Prester John. Some think the source of this story was Jinghiz Khan's early protector, Khan Toghrul of the Keraits, known by his Chinese title, Wang Khan.   He was a Nestorian Christian. Jinghiz Khan supplanted him during his rise to power.

26. This story had had an earlier currency as part of the Medieval Alexander Romance, a fictional work claiming to be a history of Alexander the Great.

27. Ruthenians: Slavs of what is now the Ukraine.

28. Carpini's catalogue of the Mongol princes' names is fairly accurate. Jinghiz's eldest son was actually named Juchi; Tossu is probably meant to be Tolui, Bati is better known as Batu, and Mengu is generally transliterated today as Mongke. He became the fourth Great Khan.

29. Commander of the Mongol army in Poland during the campaign of 1241.

30. Hubilai, or Kubilai became Great Khan and set up his capital in China where he established the Yuan Dynasty. He is the Great Khan whom the Polos visited.

31. It is interesting to note that Subotai was still living; he was the conqueror of Kwarezm under Chingis Khan and of Hungary under Batu.

32. Carpini's terms for commanders of a thousand men, a hundred men and ten men.

33. This discussion of giving horses and money to messengers refers to the *yam,* or Mongol system of post horse stations which, like the American Pony Express, was used to send mounted messengers quickly across the empire. Stations were located a few miles apart and the messengers often rode night and day, changing horses several times a day. They could demand the horse of anyone they passed, and would leave it at the next station.

34. As Carpini's word for "Sultan" is "Soldan", this must be a title rather than a name. See also, Chapter Nine where this person is mentioned again.

35. The Kumans, or Kipchaks, were a Turkic people speaking a Turkic language.

36. The campaign against the Russian principalities took place in 1236-1238.

37. Carpini's description of the battle of Mohi in 1241 is consistent with the contemporary European view that, despite the horrific result, the Mongols had somehow been fought to a draw, or would have been if the campaign had lasted longer. In fact this was not true. The Mongols abandoned Hungary after completely subjecting it because of internal political struggles.

38. In fact the Mongols destroyed Great Bolgar, a steppe city, in 1237 to pave their way for the invasion of Russia the following year.

39. Isidore of Seville (ca. 560-636) was a medieval encyclopedist who reported a number of wonders.

40. Probably a coin or unit of money.

41. Urum: the former middle eastern territories of the Byzantine Empire lost to the Muslims. The word is a corruption of "Rome".

42. This decimal ordering of soldiers is common among steppe people; according to Rachnevsky Chingis put it into effect during his war with the Naimans. See Rachnevsky, *Genghis Khan, His Life and Legacy,* Blackwell, Cambridge, Mass, 1993.

43. Carpini uses the word *tenebre*, or more properly be *tenebra,* which is Latin for "darkness". This is an unintentional pun from Mongolian. A Mongol regiment of ten thousand men was called a *tumen* which resembled another Mongol word meaning darkness.

44. The Mongol armies were very disciplined and this alone gave them an advantage over the western armies Carpini was familiar with. It is hard to believe, though, that discipline was quite as horrific as he suggests.

45. It was common for a Mongol soldier to carry a pair of bows. They were recurved composite bows of wood, horn and sinew with a maximum range over two hundred meters and an effective range of about sixty. Garlan, Y., *La Guerre dans L'Antiquite,* Fernand Nathan, Paris, 1972, pp 106-107.

46. This flexible armor, called lamellar armor, has a long history and has always been popular in Asia, and was made of leather as well. Japanese samurai armor is made this way and these days is probably the best know example of this technique.

47. By contrast European arrowheads were generally socketed.

48. This is the very tactic used by the Mongols against Bela IV and the Hungarian army at the battle of Sajo in 1241.

49. Chingis Khan, on his deathbed, is supposed to have commanded to his sons the complete conquest of the world.

50. The reference to Saxons in this context is odd since Carpini himself had been Warden of Saxony for the church and must have been familiar with the area. There does not seem to have been any incursion into Saxony proper, unless he refers to some minor foray into German territory during the invasions of Poland and Hungary in 1241, or unless he applies the term Saxon broadly to mean Germans living in settlements further east, such as at Pest in Hungary.

51. That is, submit in accordance with the terms of the letter the Khan sent with Carpini to the pope.

52. Carpini is correct in attributing the withdrawal of the Mongols from Central Europe to the death of Occodei Khan.

53. Carpini was right to warn the Europeans of this; it was the Mongol custom to either drive captives before them to help storm fortresses, or to demand of their defeated subjects that they supply them with soldiers.

54. Daniel, Prince of Galicia and Volhynia who later tried to resisted Batu by building fortresses in his territory. Batu forced him to pull them down and submit once again.

55. Russians, that is, the Orthodox Christians.

56. Bela IV had lost these to Batu in his defeat on the Sajo River in 1241.

57. Alexander Nevsky (1220?-1263), Prince of Novgorod and Russian national hero who defeated the Swedes in a battle on the Neva river and the Teutonic knights in a battle on frozen Lake Chudskoye. Despite the implication of this story, Nevsky had very good relations with the Tartars who supported him politically, making him an equivocal figure in Russian history.

58. He did this in hope that the Catholic west would send military assistance to him. This hope was never realized.

Bibliography

Benson, Douglas, S., **The Tartar War,** Maverick Publications, 1981

Brent, P., **The Mongol Empire,** Weidenfeld and Nicolson, London, 1976

Carpini, Giovanni di Plano, **Historia Mongalorum,** Centro Italiano di Studi Sull'Alto Medioevo, Spoleto, 1986

Commeaux, C., **La Vie Quotidienne Chez Les Mongols de la Conquete,** Hachette, Paris, 1972

Chambers, James, **The Devil's Horsemen,** Atheneum, N.Y., 1979

Jones, Archer, **The Art of War in the Western World,** Oxford University Press, Oxford, England, 1987

Gibbon, Edward, **The Decline and Fall of the Roman Empire,** Vols II and III, The Modern Library, N.Y. no publication date

Grousset, Rene, **The Empire of the Steppes,** N. Walford, trans., Rutgers University Press, New Brunswick, N. J., 1991

Halperin, C. J., **Russia and the Golden Horde,** Indiana University, Bloomington, Ind., 1985;
-- **The Tartar Yoke,** Slavica Publishers, Columbus Ohio, 1986

Maenchen-Helfen, O, **The World of the Huns,** University of California, Berkley 1973

Howarth, Henry H., **History of the Mongols,** Longmans, Green & Co, London, 1876

Keegan, John, **A History of Warfare,** Alfred A. Knopf, N.Y. 1993

Lamb, Harold, **Genghis Khan, Emperor of All Men,** New York, 1928 Lamb, Harold, **The March of the Barbarians,** Doubleday, Doran & Company, Inc., New York, 1940

Morgan, D., **The Mongols,** Blackwell Publishers, Cambridge, Mass, 1994

Oman, C. W. C., **The Art of War in the Middle Ages,** Cornell University Press, Ithaca, N.Y., and London, 1990

Paterson, W. F., "The Archers of Islam", **Journal of the Economic and Social History of Asia,** (1966) pp 69-87.

Prawdin, Michael, **The Mongol Empire,** E. and C. Paul, trans., Allen and Unwin Ltd, London, 1961

Rachnevsky, P., **Genghis Khan, His Life and Legacy,** T. N. Haining, trans., Blackwell Publishers, Cambridge, Mass, 1993

Sinor, D., "The Inner Asian Warriors", **Journal of the American Oriental Society,** Vol 101 (1981), pp 133-144.

INDEX